MW01075207

**WARNING:** This book contains **REAL LIFE STORIES**
that some may find **OFFENSIVE!**

# LIFE
## AS A
# JAILER

## THROUGH THE OFFICERS EYES

### WRITTEN BY:
### CAPT. JOE DEFRANCO & K-9 OFF. TOM DUNCAN

ISBN: 978-1-4834-6981-2 (sc)
ISBN: 978-1-4834-6980-5 (e)

Lulu Publishing Services rev. date: 05/24/2017

**Joe:** "To my Beautiful daughter Brooke, who could not be more loved."
Dad

**Tom:** "To my wife Lorre & two sons, Tom & Mike; you guys are my world, I love you."

# ACKNOWLEDGEMENTS

We would like to thank:

~ Front Cover Paid for & Gifted by: ~
Daniel Del Valle from **NJ Blue Now Magazine**
www.NJBlueNow.com
973.653.3446

&

For their blurbs on the back cover:

**BERNARD B. KERIK** - Police Commissioner City of New York (retired)

**Anthony Gangi** - Host of Tier Talk / CorrectionsOne

**Daniel Del Valle** - NJ BLUE NOW MAGAZINE EDITOR-IN-CHIEF

# PROLOGUE

In this book, we hope to give you a true knowledge of what really goes on behind the bars in a prison and/or jail. First, due to the nature of its content, all readers of this book should be at least 18 years old. We really don't hold **anything** back.

At one time or another, almost everybody has wondered what goes on inside a prison or jail. Many have some concepts or ideas from television but they truly don't know what really goes on. For that reason, we will share our stories that will enlighten people to the dangers, realities, and truths of the on-goings behind the bars. Believe us, it's a tell-all book and we're not holding back anything.

We will give you a true understanding of what Correctional Officers go through on a daily basis at work and how it also affects them at home. Hopefully, you'll have a new respect for all Correctional Officers after you've finished reading this book, because in our mind "No job is more dangerous or more thankless than a Correctional Officer's."

**Note:** FYI- Some chapters were written by Joe, some by Tom and some we wrote together. We just wanted to give you a heads-up to this, because we didn't want to confuse you with the way we bounced back and forth through-out the book with the use of different personal pronouns.

Left to Right (retired): Captain Joe DeFranco, Commissioner N.Y.P.D. Bernard B Kerik & K-9 Officer Tom Duncan

The picture above was taken the night we met with Commissioner Kerik, and asked him to review our book (see blurb on the back cover.)

Not only was Mr. Kerik both, Corrections & Police Commissioner of New York City, he is also a New York Times Bestselling Author and an overall GREAT guy! Mr. Kerik is a wealth of information; we got some very valuable tips from him that night on marketing & "tuning-up" our book.

Joe and I are now proud to be able to call him a friend.

# TABLE OF CONTENTS

# ABOUT THE AUTHOR'S

**Captain Joe DeFranco:** Well my Law Enforcement career started in 1987 as an officer for the Passaic County Sheriff's Department in New Jersey. I attended the Morris County Police Academy in 1988. During my 25 year career, I've performed many jobs in the jail facility including, Gang Unit Director, Classification Director, worked in the reception area. In 1996 I was promoted to Sergeant and in 2000 promoted to Lieutenant. In 2001 I was again promoted to Captain all after taking the civil service promotional exams. For the next 10 years I served as the Shift Commander for all 3 shifts in the jail. In 2011 I was assigned as an Administrative Captain overseeing all shifts. My passion from years 2003 until I retired in 2013 was being and serving as the PBA 197 Superior Officers' President which afforded me the opportunity to help many officers and brass. I have no regrets having worked with the hardest working professionals in the business. I will always call any Corrections Officer anywhere in the Country a true hero. God Bless America!

**K-9 Officer Tom Duncan**: I was forced to retire from a Sheriff's Department in Northern New Jersey for medical reasons, back in November of 2000. An on-the-job injury left me permanently and totally disabled from performing the functions of a Law-Enforcement Officer. Prior to working in New Jersey as a Corrections Officer, I worked for a Sheriff's Department down in southern Florida as a Corrections Officer on the maximum-security floor of the jail. In the twelve short years I've worked as a corrections officer, I attended two corrections academies and one police K-9 Academy. I've been in numerous physical altercations. I've had things thrown at me that I wouldn't even touch let alone pick up myself and throw at someone. I was credited with extinguishing a fire inside a jail unit and saving the lives of 24 inmates. I've seen things that no human being should ever have to see. I've worked with some GREAT officers and I've worked with some... well, let's just leave it with I've work with some GREAT officers. I've worked in departments where officers have been killed and inmates have escaped. Looking back at my career, there are many things I would change if I could. One thing for certain that I wouldn't change is, working with some of the BEST Law-Enforcement Officers ever. May GOD continue to bless all who have walked the walk; past, present and future.

# CHAPTER 1

## It's Time To Get Real

OK here comes the $64,000 question. So what is the MAIN reason for violence in a correctional institution? OK before you start thinking too hard about this let me say that, that was somewhat of a rhetorical question. Because there really isn't just one MAIN reason for violence.

A violent act can occur over something as simple as just a look one prisoner or inmate gives another. There are so many things that can be contributed as a motivating factor for violence but one of the biggest has to do with gang activity. Gang activity plays a major role when it comes to violence and the reasons can range from something like a rules violation within the gang to a conflict with another gang.

So to say some times gangs prey on their own is evident almost every day inside the walls. I can remember a night where we were called to a cell dorm that housed a certain gang. The call was that a fight was in progress and a large group of inmates had congregated to the back of the dorm.

As soon as I heard that I knew this would be big trouble because I knew they huddle in the back like that so the cameras couldn't see what they are doing. When the back-up team arrived it was discovered that one inmate had been assaulted.

And how he was assaulted was just horrible. They held him down, took boiling scalding water and poured it onto his face until the point that his skin started peeling off his face. By the time we got to him, he was in obvious shock. Seeing this type of violence has not only a profound effect on the staff but also the inmates who aren't involved. This inmate had burns like I've never seen before and was immediately rushed to the burn unit. Later during the investigation it was discovered that the gang he was in called him out as a rat and this was in retribution for him talking.

This just goes to show that gangs in prisons and jails, right or wrong take actions not only on other gang members but also on their own members. And you can only imagine that if they can do something like that to one of their own; there's no telling what they can and will do to anyone else.

Brutal attacks like this happen very often in all correctional institutions around this country and it's something you can get used to, but when it is this brutal it's very hard to forget.

But what it comes down to is this: It's just another day at work for the Corrections Officer

(Once you've heard the sound of cell doors slamming shut, it's a sound that will never leave your mind...)

Growing up, if you would have told me, I'd spend twenty five years of my life in a jail working as a Corrections Officer; I'd say, "You're out of your mind." Well, that's in fact exactly how my life played out. Now I know many people think that you would have to be a bit crazy to do that job as a living, and maybe, just maybe they're justifiably right in thinking that. But as you will see more importantly it's a job that not only did my coworkers and I take great pride in, it's a job that we took very seriously (and I mean Life and Death serious, at times) because as you should know it's like no other job in the world. I will tell you this much, it's definitely a job that is full of seeing and being involved in many things, from the littlest things, to very violent acts, and all being done without much praise by the community.

This is a story that not many who have ("walked the walk") will talk about, but yet is a story that many people are intrigued about hearing. Thus is one of the biggest reasons why and what prompted us to write this book.

Although by no means is the life of a jail guard a pretty one, and when I say I was a jail guard, you should know it's a term we called ourselves, but to the public we prefer the term Corrections Officer because we are a group of professionals, highly trained and it's a sign of respect.

I learned early in my career that started back in the early nineteen eighties, that there were very few people who lived in my community that would even want this job; I might add, or as a matter of fact any community in the U.S.A. But for some strange reason, I decided to start this journey that would take me in many directions, good, bad and even sometimes ugly.

Now if you've watched any television shows or movies depicting a jail or prison setting, you would think that there are many similarities in the way things happen and the way things are done. And although there are many, there really isn't (now I know that's an oxymoron) but it's true. Hopefully by the end of this book I'll be able to clear that statement up for you so it makes sense.

One of the first things Corrections Officers (A.K.A. CO's) are trained to do is to refrain from seeing the crime that was committed by the inmate and to treat all of them the same. Well, I can tell you first hand that as human beings that's one of if not the hardest things to do. Especially knowing what some of these scumbags (oh I'm sorry, I mean inmates) are arrested for and then convicted of. And I would challenge anyone to try and keep their personal opinions and actions out of their mindset, and how it affects them doing this job while like working with an animal that you know has raped a child.

It's a job that has just as many mental conflicts as well as physical conflicts and thus the reason why many officers turn to alcohol and drugs in their daily life. Even keeping their life at work private about all the many things that go on, even from their family, that love them.

Hopefully, this book will give you somewhat of a "REAL" window to look into so you can see what "we" as CO's call just another day at work.

Okay so now I'll tell you just how this "Life as a Jailer" starts off. After deciding that working in a jail is what you want to do, one of the first things that happens is what I like to call "It's time to get REAL" you're given a tour of the jail facility. Later on, you find out that this is where many prospective "jailers" decide that this is not really something that's going to be a possible career for them. And even if you can get past the initial small hard looks from the inmates and an occasional wiseass remark, then it's time for your two weeks (in house) training.

Now truly for the first time in your life you're in a jail, and believe me when I tell you this; there's nothing that can prepare you for what you'll see over those next two weeks. For the first time you get a small (TRUE) idea of what this job is really all about.

Two of the first things that are noticed right off the bat, are all the inmates walking around in their boxers with headphones on like they're at one big party and have no care in the world, and that God awful horrible smell in the air, that at first almost makes you feel like you're going to get sick, and all because the large percentage of these inmates have no hygiene skills and could care less! Over those next two weeks of "in house" training. The training officer goes over many things and once in the Corrections

Academy you learn even a hell of a lot more. But what it really all comes down to is this: Working in a jail is all about teamwork with your fellow officers and having their backs. It's always about getting home after your shift. And even though you know your other officers have your back and will be there to help you out, it could feel like forever before they actually get to you in an emergency. "Back in the day," as I like to say now, we the old timers often only had one line of defense against attacks (until our backup arrived) from the so called residents of the jail, and that being and most importantly our own fighting skills, something that would and could end up being the only difference between getting home safely that day or not.

Not like the jails of today. Where officers are equipped with state of the art OC spray in cans (**Pepper spray,** also known as **OC spray** from "oleoresin capsicum" this OC gas was developed in the early 1980's by the Zarc International Company. Which introduced a proprietary "capsicum pepper technology" to be used as a safe and effective non-lethal weapon by the military and law enforcement officers. It didn't actually make it into most of the jails until the late 90's. F.Y.I.- "Capsicums" are chili peppers which come in many varieties and range from mild to hot. Capsicum encompasses twenty species and some 300 different varieties of pepper plants.) Believe me when I tell you, once you've been sprayed, with it, it burns like hell. You can't even force your eyes to open. It completely disables you from doing anything. Now this can also be shot out of guns. In some states today, officers also have tasers and a team of ready-made trained officers that are suited for inmate extractions. They can employ some every cool modern day tools that they have available to use.

I remember my first day at work, fresh out of the academy. Standing on my first post, which of course was patrolling maximum security. When an inmate walked up to the bars, looked me straight in the eyes like he was pissed off and said, "What in the fuck do you think is so funny." I looked at him, and I'm not ashamed to say, I was a bit scared that day, even though we had bars in between us and I said, "I don't think anything is funny." still scared, the inmate looked at me and smiled and said, "Got you man, I'm just playing with you." You see he knew, I was new "a rookie" and to be honest with you inmates know just about everything that's going on in their "world" which is the jail. Especially their immediate surroundings and a lot know even what's happening on other wings of the jail.

Your mindset in this job plays a big roll on the effects the job will have on your life and career! Many people who start this career have no idea just like the public what they're in for when they start this journey as a CO. An open mindset is essential and if you're going to stay sane during your career. It's important to keep an even keel and not get to wound up in the emotional aspect and personal attacks you may be subject to from time to time. And I'm not just talking from the inmates.

You can go many days in the jail without any incidents from the population; but on the many days you do/will have them, it can be extremely draining both physically and mentally. That going home after a shift or going out with the "Guys for a few cold ones!" as you will find out happens way too often and though it's a great release from the stress of the job, it can be a very bad detriment to your family life.

Many times CO's get home not only half in the bag, because of this reason, but if they do have a family they tend to keep what happened that day on that shift, private from their significant other. Thus because we (CO's) sometimes feel or think that we (our Correction Officer's family) are the only people who will really understand what happened that day. So being single and working as a CO can at times be a lot easier on the stress and anxiety this job will bring into your life. So right or wrong we keep it from everyone except for ourselves.

Later on in my career as I looked back on it, holding these things in and not talking about them was very detrimental and definitely the wrong approach. Going out almost every night after a shift, as you can imagine, might feel good at the time and feeling like it's a big stress and anxiety release. But it's only compounding the problem and besides having a badge and going out drinking is never a good idea, though some would disagree.

Now when I said personal attacks remember I wasn't just talking about it coming from the inmate population. It also comes from the public, the administration you work for and the government agency that you work for. Yes, I'll say it, sometimes the biggest stress and anxiety you'll ever have comes from your own administration and co-workers rather than the inmate population. You see, the inmates for the most part need you and comply with most orders, but political games in the department can be devastating to some and great for others. That's something you really don't have any control over. All you can do is always keep that even keel about yourself while working your shift, because you're always going to be tested by and not only by the inmate population in the jail. You need to watch your every move with these inmates and what you say they get plenty information about you as it is. You may say, "How is that possible?" Well because many other officers walk around talking about their lives and yours with other officers and the inmates are always listening. My advice would be, as hard as it seems to do, to never talk about your personal life in front of anyone at work and where you are going to meet the guys after work.

Working at night and getting out at around that midnight hour brought out another whole aspect of the job. In the early part of an officer's career that can become the start of a long road and for some officers, which will lead into some very bad results.

Of course, going out with the guys always sounds good at first and helps relieve some of the stress of the day. Having a few drinks sounded very appealing especially when you're the new guy on the block and you want to make friends.

The only problem, going out with the guys at work is that it never stopped at just a few and lasts well into the morning hours and this happens all too frequently. I will say this, and it should be a "given" not many good things happen to people that are drinking at that hour of the morning. And many times people (Officers) drive that shouldn't be (they have that, I have a Badge syndrome). If there was a top ten list for this old timer that I could magically put into the heads of every new officer this would be real close to the top: Never Drink and Drive, period!!! And always have a person drive who is not drinking with you, or have alternate transportation home. This advice will probably save your career and God forbid, the life of yourself or someone else.

Now that being said, as I hope all of you are aware of the "FACT" that not every officer or co-worker can be trusted, and I've worked with a few. They know who they are and in a later chapter I may name names just for fun!

So if you decide "It's time to get REAL" then keep in mind it's a job that's thankless and the only pat on the back you'll ever get is from your coworkers who are sweating alongside you and know what you're going through every day. You'll work with men and women who we call the unsung heroes of Law Enforcement because we go where not many will even think to go. Face to face with the most violent criminals in the country who for some could care less about our lives or care if we get home at night. Also remember that this job has the following: many assaults on staff by inmates, on average two serious assaults will happen to you in a twenty year career, on average a CO lives only eighteen months after retirement, and 31% of CO's in America suffer from PTSD according to a report by Desert Waters Correctional Outreach! So would you be willing to work alongside the bravest group of individuals in the country we know and who we have the utmost respect for?

Since there is no closing time in the jail it's open 24/7/365 days a year, thus three different shifts are need to run it. Now working at night for some isn't a normal thing, especially if you have kids and a family. You go to work at 3pm and get out at 11pm and you rarely see your family, it can cause many problems for your domestic life and also lead to bad behavior even for a strong-willed person.

I've said many times to people that work in a jail, this place makes good people do bad things, which they would not normally do. The normal stress level at times can be overwhelming and the 3pm to 11pm shift multiplies that stress. This is why most officers prefer the day shifts 7am to 3pm.

Now working the midnight shift 11pm to 7am is a whole separate animal to deal with. Personally, I loved that shift and the people, and will always have great memories working with those hard working dedicated officers. Sometimes the officers working on this shift are looked down upon by their own department. The officers I worked with on the 11pm to 7am shift took it personally and decided they would prove to everyone in the department how these so called step children of the department could be the best of the best. These officers trained for every specialty unit offered. They were tops in Swat (Special Weapons And Tactics), Bomb Squad, K-9 Unit, Sort (Special Operations Response Team.) I'm proud to have been part of this shift as the Shift Commander for around 6 years of my career. The worst thing about working the 3pm to 11pm & 11pm to 7am shifts is "Sleep Deprivation!" Many of the officers I've worked with and myself included have slept less than 4 hours a day for periods of a time and at times even went 48 hours without sleep.

# CHAPTER 2

*Fighting A Two Front War*

One thing that remains the same within every jail is that inmates have twenty four hours a day seven days a week (the street slang is 24/7) to watch us (Corrections Officers) do our job and in some cases watch officers who aren't doing their jobs, and to try and figure out how to beat you out of whatever their scam is and that can range from getting an extra dinner roll to planning an escape or riot. This is what I would later in my career call the first front war.

Now what's not always the same in each jail, and is something I had also learned later in my career and is what I liked to call the second front war. Now you should know that this war is and can be just as bad as the first, even sometimes worse. Which unfortunately turned out to be useful advice that I could rarely give to a new officer and couldn't even talk about it, out loud.

This was the so called unwritten rules that were implemented for the sole protection of the governmental agency who was in charge of the jail and had nothing really to do with officer safety which quite frankly they couldn't really care less about.

When you work for a department that is like a feared Roman Empire and even a local newspaper is using that as a similar quote to run a special series addition. And you know that as an officer everything they're writing about is true and if you don't, you will quickly learn that there are many unwritten rules to adhere to if you are going to survive in this career without having to fight this two front war daily. Our Sheriff along with his Deputy One Sheriff ran that department like a mini Adolf Hitler camp.

The only thing they truly worried about was maintaining their positions of power and this paradigm came at a costly price for many individuals if you weren't onboard during campaigning time for elections or attending dinners for fundraisers you were ostracized and targeted by the administration. They would come at you with a fierce vengeance trying to destroy you in any way they could even if the consequences were you losing your (Job) position as an officer and ruining your family life. This was truly the second front of the war that we needed to fight on a daily basis, besides having to deal with the inmates.

So now imagine having to come to work in a jail not only having to worry about murders, rapists and such; but having to worry about what political party you endorsed! I'm sure many of you know a little something about this.

How about coming to work and having someone ask you why you're not displaying a Sheriffs bumper sticker on your car, and it was another officer asking? Imagine another officer walking around with a clipboard with names on it, asking if you're buying a ticket for a fundraiser or if you're showing up for a parade. You'd probably would say yes, if it meant you wouldn't have to be followed around at work and knowing "Big Brother" is watching every move you made, because if you didn't that it would be scrutinized by someone who was handpicked by the administration to make sure you're aware of the consequence of not being onboard and not following those unwritten rules! Imagine if you've seen others who were targeted for this reason and may have lost their livelihoods and career?

But then again if you were in good graces with that administration and played the "GAME" you prospered. Although for the very few who will do what they feel is right they were looked upon as lepers to their coworkers. So many did comply, but imagine the stress this caused for many good people who in this department just wanted to really go to work and go home to their families at the end of each work day.

Eventually every Empire falls, but there's always someone else next in line that's promising to make changes and eliminating the "rat" mentality. But decades of a culture is hard to change even if the best of intentions are started. Inside politics and a lack of seniority being honored will kill the moral and spirit of an organization, do everything you can to prevent this.

Before we get into this chapter any further I would just like to make one thing very clear. As Correction Officers (both in Prisons & Jails) we face almost every aspect of the job the same, with the exception of how strong politics comes into play. As we all know or should know there are Correction Officers that work for Sheriff's Departments and Correction Officers that work for the State. Well let's just say that politics, as far as politicians playing a bigger role in the day to day running of a correctional facility it's a lot more influential in this career within a Sheriff's Department.

Many years ago, when I first started my career as a Corrections Officer I never imagined having to deal with the amount of political <u>bullshit</u> that I had to endure with to the point where it would ruin the morale and many alleged friendships at our facility! From officers that are in the so called "circle of trust" with the current boss, running around and allowed to do less work, tell stories about their co-workers, true and most times false, and creating a animosity within a department that had many more pressing concerns to deal with. Not to even mention the biggest problem of all; come time for elections. The tension between the current boss and his supporters and the officers who go against the current boss and do what is their "Constitutional Right" and support the opponent in the election. I've seen many times officers who are friends for years become enemies over this and at times it has turned physical. Now in the Sheriff's Department Tom and I worked at there is no need to mention names because everyone reading this who knows us, knows who we're talking about.

Just stop and think for a moment what it would be like to have that added presser put on you, on top of all the normal stress a Corrections Officer has to endure. Can you even imagine working for a department as an officer; where there is and are individuals whose job it is to tell the boss who his opponent's supporters on the job are? Then the top administrators telling the shift supervisors who they are so they can be targeted on their posts, and at times even trying to ruining the good careers of officers who have earned everything they've gotten! I'm sure every Corrections Officer who has ever worked or works for a Sheriff's Department knows what I'm talking about. We all have had them; officers (and I use that word officers in this case very loosely) who's only job it is, is to run errands for the boss and make sure he's elected time and time again!

If one of the only things I can accomplish by writing this book it's my hope that I can change the mentality of the officers who work in departments like this that they stay far and clear from the politics and the politicians! Just go to work and do your job and go home to your families. WOW... wouldn't that be a novel idea!

I've always said, if the Rats in your/my department were ousted and shunned by the rest of the good guys, and maybe taken outside to the back of the jail and have a stern talking to. Maybe this type of stuff wouldn't go on! But because we love our jobs and don't want to lose them we try to do things the right way, but as we all know being the nice guy around low life people doesn't always turn out the way we want it to and we're forced to work in environments like this.

I would just like to remind everyone and for those who don't know, educate; on how big of a role politics, or should I say politicians, play in County Government. The Sheriff's Department falling under the auspice of the county freeholders thus falls victim to this time and time again, is of particular concern.

As everyone knows a sheriff's department budget takes a big bite out of county tax money. Thus putting it on top of a short list of ways to help balance the budget. But in order to do that these freeholders need to make decisions on how County money is spent and where cutbacks can be made. Now I'm sure anyone reading this who knows or had any experience in the past with any politician can attest to the fact that 99.9% of them are little lying weasels, and will do or say anything to get elected.

Now these County freeholders are no different than any other politician. They become very friendly with everyone around them during election time, and because a sheriff's department can and in most cases do have a large number of employees. They tend to turn to them for help in getting elected or reelected. In a political sense this is a very smart move especially for an incumbent. They know they'll have many volunteers; some individuals whose motives may be sparked by visions of advancement or just by someone who want to stay on the right side of the bosses and not be targeted as a non-supporter.

Okay with that said I would like to give you an example of how this just might play out. Quick story, one year during election time this little weasel of a politician came around asking for help like he did every three years, and did in fact ended up with many volunteers who wanted to help out there boss/bosses out. Well this politician in question ended up winning the election. So what do you think happen next; just a mere two weeks after the election?

Well the little weasel of a guy that he is, decided it was time to start massive layoffs within the sheriff's department in order to try and balance the budget. A budget he now wanted to balance by firing the same people who he had no problem going to for help two weeks earlier in hopes of getting reelected to a freeholder's seat. As if corrections officers don't have enough to worry about while on the job now they need to start worrying about the very men they helped get elected. A man who not only at that time wanted to cut back the security of the County jail, making it even a bigger ticking time bomb and harder place to work. He eventually went on to establish a political platform to close the jail in a horrible attempt in what he called shared services with other counties. Shared services to him meant the loss of 400 jobs and careers of officers who worked and lived and pay taxes within his county. These funds now freely to flow how he saw fit.

The one thing this politician did wrong other than having an ill-conceived plan was taking for granted the tenacity of the correction officers who he was throwing to the dogs. These corrections officers with the help of many supporters within the community were able to stop the madness thank God, by bringing to light to the voters of the county that this ill-conceived plan was nothing more than a smokescreen that would give these county politicians more power and funds to do with as they pleased to secure their own political gains. All under the pretense that they were going to balance a budget and save the tax payer a dime. The one thing that bothers me the most about that story is knowing that stories like this go on within every sheriff's department across the country. I have a sneaking suspicion this idea will raise its ugly head again within our own county.

Here is a quick story that's even worse than this last. We had several officers who would attend union/ PBA meetings that were being held for contract negotiations and running information back to the politicians. The same politicians mind you who were trying to slice our department apart. Talk about having a Judas Iscariot among your midst; not surprising but heartbreaking. Thus we needed to stop these talks among the ranks making everyone upset but only in the best interest of those members were talks continued and discussed just among committee members. You see at times we are our own worst enemy.

**A Statement from Joe**: Enclosing this chapter I would like to add the answer to a fun question I get all the time from people who I talk to, especially after they find out I was a Corrections Officer for 25 years and retired as an Administrative Captain of a large Sheriff's Department in New Jersey.

That question is "If you were ever a Sheriff of any Department how would you run it?" I start out by telling them that foremost I would be a real SHERIFF and NOT a POLITICIAN because to be truthfully honest with you, I hate politicians, they're all liars. Then I'd tell them I would trim out all the bullshit fat (And I'm not talking about services that would affect the citizens) from the Sheriff's Department that's eating up their taxpaying dollars and put it to better use. The people of my County would know that they deserve nothing less, then the highest standards from the Sheriff's Department. I would ensure that the Sheriff's Department would perform at the HIGHEST professional level expected by all the citizens of the county. I also would ensure and guarantee that crime would go down, by attacking violent crime, gangs and the ongoing drug problems within the county with the tenacity of a lion on the hunt for food. In doing so every citizen would be reassured daily that they have a Sheriff that has their daily safety in mind as his #1 priority & will never let them forget it.

The most important thing (I would do) for the Officers of that Department would happen behind the proverbial curtain of the department; that would be to make a **REAL PROMISE** (And I FUCKING mean REAL) to all the officers of that Sheriff's Department and that would be this: For the first time **EVER** (if you vote for me) you will have a Sheriff who is committed to providing **REAL** support to the Officers of this Sheriff's Department & also running it in a **FAIR WAY**, without all the Bull-Shit all the other Sheriff's let go on by their Undersheriffs & Wardens. I would tell them that they would have **MY WORD** that all the Bull-Shit that has gone on there before **WILL END** the very first day I take over.

And to drive all of that home, and to make sure everyone knows I'm for real making these statements. I would NOT even accept a salary; my first year as Sheriff and would donate all that money to charities within the county...

That's just the tip of the iceberg of what a Sheriff Joe DeFranco would be all about... (A no nonsense tough as hell crime fighter & you'd heard the saying "he's a Cops Cop" well I'd be a **TRUE** Sheriff Officer's Sheriff.)

# CHAPTER 3

## *Violence, A Way Of Life*

Imagine having to go to work every day and experiencing the threat of violence, verbal abuse, and horrible conditions? Well for many Correction Officers that's just a normal day at work. Confrontations with the inmate population is an everyday fact for us and has to be dealt with professionally and in a swift manor.

You see in our profession there's no losing a fight and that's because the system will break down. You have to draw a fine line between being professional under constant verbal abuse and at times assaults by the inmate population and standing firm under stress. Yes, there are times many years ago and I'm sure to a degree today that officers have to decide how to handle a tense situation by using justifiable force with your hands as you wait for help. Can you even imagine being confronted by an inmate or inmates looking for trouble and you having to fight for your life?

(Does the front of the building you work at look like this? There's a reason Joe & I can make statements like: Correction Officers have the most dangerous job in the world; because this is what ours looks like...)

Well it's all too often true for Correction Officers all over this country. How we handle these situations makes us the professionals we are and how to avoid them is even more important and a valuable tool in our job. To do that, we need to think ahead before we make any moves, you see it's not all about being physical 100% of the time at work, I like to say "Work smarter, not harder." In this profession of ours we don't just get paid for the job we do, we get paid for the things that can go wrong and the things we stop before they even happen!

Witnessing violent assaults on inmates by other inmates is all too common to us and as an officer it is our job to keep the population safe sometimes breaking up these violent acts. That's why every officer has to have the assurance that his fellow officers have his back, under every instance that these assaults occur. A fast response to a fellow officers need for "Back-Up" is essential and I've found this to be the most important thing in these situations. Remember, it's a very dangerous place to work at for the whole staff.

Being in a constant state of fight or flight many officers over the years can't deal with the stress of the job and the violence anymore. Post-traumatic Stress Disorder (PTSD) is not only something a soldier gets who has been in war. It's a mental health condition that effects CO's also, from very mild cases and symptoms to being debilitating. It's usually triggered or follows by an experience or witnessing of a terrifying, tragic or traumatic event in that Correction Officers life while at work. Because of this, the divorce rate among this profession is much higher than the average citizen's job. Symptoms can include and range from depression to persistent frightening thoughts, flashbacks, nightmares and severe anxiety, as well as uncontrollable thoughts about the event and feeling emotionally numb, especially with people they were once close to. PTSD for a fact and also depression in this field is unequaled by any other profession. Officers have been spit at, punched, kicked and beaten so badly with weapons like pipes, they been burned, stabbed by shanks, and some have even lost their lives. All in what would be called a day at work, just doing their job trying to keep the public safe by insuring (What I call the three C's) the jails: Custody, Care and Control of some of the worse (animals alive, I mean) inmates incarcerated.

On top of all that it's a profession that gets very few accolades from the public or cops on the street for that matter, if they only knew and the only way that would ever be possibly is to "Walk the Walk, CO's do every day!"

I will say this; that not all inmates are bad and want to cause harm to the staff, but that's the only good news. The bad news is: that more violent offenders are coming to jail, and the mental health of plenty of inmates in this country is alarming.

Imagine being at work and having feces thrown at you, or having an inmate refuse to leave his cell covering himself in his own feces? Something many people are reluctant and find it too disgusting to even talk about but is something that is a common event in our lives while at work.

Here's a pleasant thought for you; reoccurring acts of violence and frequency is much higher with each gang member that's arrested and added to the jails count. How about having to deal with this; one inmate throwing boiling water on the face of another inmate because they deem him a rat! I've personally witnessed a man's head being slammed into a metal table and had his forehead crushed wide open and lived. How about a man having a heart attack and dying in his cell after having an altercation with another inmate.

All too often Daily trips need to be made to the emergency room (E.R.), the extent of the injuries vary from, broken jaws, cuts to the face requiring stitches, burns, broken hands, I hope you're starting to get the picture here!

(High security inmates are handcuffed behind their back and shacked at the ankles; anytime they're removed from their cells...)

To say that a jail is one of the most violent workplaces to work at in this country is a "HUGE" understatement and it's not only inmates that take that ride to the hospital E.R. Officers lose their careers everyday caused by injuries either from assaults from inmates or from helping a weaker inmate that's getting abused by another inmate! Many friends have had to sit home injured and their careers destroyed. Here is only just one example of that: I saw an officer get his finger bit right off while trying to stop a fight between two inmates!

Working in a jail, officers are challenged every day, and have to remain professional and vigilant at all times, even in the face of being threated, ridicule and various other kinds of assaults from the inmate population.

I must also stress that by no means does this mean you have to endure any physical or verbal assaults from inmates. Remaining professional and justifiable defending yourself when need be, this is the key to insure not only your only safety but sends out a signal to all the inmate that you're an officer that plays by the book and takes no shit and make sure you document everything. Many officers in this line of work will tell you to keep a copy of every single report you ever write and it's not a bad idea to keep a personal diary. This is what is meant by, and what we officers call CYA (Cover Your Ass.)

I can't stress enough, especially in today's climate, where the A.C.L.U. (American Civil Liberties Union) and other liberal organizations have blamed officers for everything from assaults and many other allegations based solely on the word on an inmate and without realizing that these inmates have everything to gain and VERY little to lose. That's why when cameras were finally implemented in most of the jails across the country and started recording; it served as a great tool against any false allegations by the inmates.

Most civilians and even some inmates are not aware of this but there's a rule by law which law-enforcement officers are covered under, known as the escalation of physical and deadly force which simply means when an officer is in a confrontation he is allowed to not only meet whatever force he is met by with the same force but he can escalate it one step higher in order to defend himself or anyone else. With that in mind we must also remember that many inmates will try and bait you into an altercation, this is where being a professional pays off, we must not let this occur. Remember document everything and don't take anything personal, even though this may be hard in the beginning of your career.

Not being used to getting disrespected, many rookie officers will want to use physical force when it's not needed. That's where the help of the older, more experienced officer plays a vital role in the development of the younger officers. As veterans you learn to not take the words of an inmate to heart and remain strong and professional and you will go home every night with a clear head and less stress. Many times I've had to stop myself and others from this mistake and we don't get enough credit for the restraint we use in many stressful situations. All you ever hear about are the mistakes made, never the majority of situations we squash before they get ugly!

Remember if you're that officer who plays by the book 100% and professional this will ensure that any liberal groups that are looking to sue you or have you put on trial that their case will have no to very little merit.

If I were asked to reinforce just one point to every new rookie on the job and was told I can only use one sentence to do it. I'd say, "Complacency can get you KILLED in this profession." One definition of this word reads as followed: A feeling of quiet pleasure or security, often while unaware of some potential danger, defect, or the like; self-satisfaction or smug-satisfaction with an existing situation, condition, ect... Here is a perfect example of that: There was a veteran officer I worked with who was a K-9 officer, while questioning an inmate one day (and for reasons, which GOD only knows) this officer secured his K-9 to a fence. Now the only reason I can come up with for him breaking procedure is, complacency. This officer must have had at least 15 years on the job and was a K-9 officer for the last 4 years. He must have also questioned hundreds of inmates while being just a K-9 officer in that time period. Well that act of complacency on that day killed him. The inmate who was a trustee working under this officer's supervision outside the Jail had a plan that day, that this officer was totally unaware of. You see this inmate knew how this officer would react to him because it wasn't the first time they worked on a detail together. Basically what it came down to is this; this inmate tested this officer in the past and worked his plan out around that. What happened was while working one day this inmate started a verbal confrontation with the officer and escalated it to the point where the inmate told the officer the only reason he has the balls to talk to him like that was because he had a dog. So the officer trying to prove to this inmate that he was man enough to stand toe to toe with him, he tied his dog off. That's when this inmates plan for his escape went into full effect, so with a handful of dirt that the K-9 officer could not see that the inmate had. He threw it in the officer's face, then punched him in the throat, grabbed his weapon and shot him. "Complacency cannot just maybe get you KILLED in this profession, it will." And unfortunately you don't have to be a rookie, most of the officers I've seen who were complacent were veterans. FYI- this inmate was captured within twenty four hours after his escape and when questioned on why he did what he did. He told investigators he had to because he need to see his girlfriend to straighten out a problem and that he really liked that officer and was sorry for having to kill him.

After a few years on the job a Corrections Officer starts to develop a keen sense of awareness to his environment at work. A sense of awareness that only becomes sharper and sharper as the years increase on the job. Certain signals he looks for in the inmate population, you probably would be surprised to know this but a very large percentage of veteran officers can read the inmate population the way you're reading this book. I guess you can call it an instinctive feel for what's going on or what is about to happen or may happen.

As a Correction Officer you learn very early in your career that shit can kick off at any time. Whether it's between an inmate and staff or inmate an inmate. So developing a sense and ability to read the inmates in the population is a great tool that the officer must learn to develop through his career, one that can and maybe just will save his own life one day.

The signals, signs, and vibes that come off the inmate population can vary, from as simple or slight as one inmate's surreptitious nod to another or to as obvious as an inmate running directly at another inmate yelling.

I'll tell you from personal experience one thing that scares an officer the most, maybe I shouldn't say scares, concerns him the most is a better way to put it. Is when things go quiet, or there feels like there's a peace, a sense of tranquility, almost like the saying "The quiet before the storm." The silents sometimes is so strong and deafening you can feel it in your bones as a veteran officer you're sure something's ready to kick off.

You have to remember violence is a way of life for these inmate/prisoners it's how they earned their stripes out on the streets and its how they earn their respect inside the walls and behind the bars. And the more violent and apathetic an inmate/prisoner is the more respect is given by his fellow peers, it's also how these guys climb the ladder of power within their gangs.

I would have to say a greater percentage of the violent acts within a correctional facility are spontaneous. And can vary from a simple thing as I didn't like the way he was looking at me and/or to just wanting to prove to someone else that you're not someone to be fucked with. Planned assaults are usually and most likely because of revenge or gang related. Either way both could have the same deadly results. As a matter fact the more severe and brutal the violence or the attack is the better the inmate prisoners see it and respects it.

Many times when called upon for help, Correction officers are fast and like a wild group who comes in charging like the U.S. Calvary and most of the time not even 100% sure of knowing what they're getting into and for that we both tip our hats to all the courageous Correction Officers "Past and Present" in all the jails and prisons across this country and especially the ones we've worked with. This I can tell you without any reservations, both Tom and I were always there ready to risk our lives when another officer needed help.

# CHAPTER 4

## No Respect, No Thanks...

One of the main reasons for writing this book was to bring to light the fact that Correction Officers are the unsung TRUE heroes in law-enforcement.

It's a well-known fact by all Corrections Officers that they go unnoticed, unappreciated and they're looked down upon not only by the general public, but also by their peers in law-enforcement; from prosecutors all the way down to street cops. Even in most movies they're portrayed as being stupid, lazy and incompetent. And lot of these individuals who look down on this profession are under the belief that a large percentage of Correction Officers only became Correction Officers because they couldn't become "a real cop".

It's unfortunate that this paradigm is a stigma that Correction Officers must work under and are viewed as such, especially by their peers in law-enforcement. Who should know better!

Even a large percentage of the general public fails to see the Corrections Officer as the professionals they are within the law-enforcement community. Most people just referred to them as Jail Guards or glorified babysitters. This persona must change and credit, respect and gratitude must be given where it's deserved.

Now I don't want anyone to take this the wrong way and I'm not trying to belittle the danger our counterparts in law-enforcement (The street cop) may incur while on the job. Did everyone just understand what I wrote there? Go back and read this paragraph again, by no means am I saying that Police Officers do not put their life's at risk to protect our communities. I'm just trying to make a point to the ethics and courage that makes up the Corrections Officer. Sadly a majority of both the community and our counterparts do not realize that Correction Officers do the same thing but only on a much higher percentage of times each day.

With all that said, let me be as bold to put the facts on the table. Police officers ride around in a patrol car with a 9mm strapped to their waste and a shotgun only an arm's length away. And most of the time, at any one given time are dealing with only one to maybe four individuals. And a large percentage of these individuals they're dealing with for the most part are law abiding citizens breaking minor motor vehicle violations, or they're called on medical emergencies, very few times in his career does a police officer encounter a felon or are put into a position where he needs to use physical force to effect an arrest. The facts are that there are many police officers throughout this country that can go their whole career without even using their handcuffs even one time. Now I would be remorse if I did not acknowledge that there are many police officers who work in high crime cities or inner city areas that need to confront violent and dangerous situations almost daily. I'm speaking about the larger percentages of the police officers in this country that make up the majority, who work in rural and suburban areas.

Whereas a good majority of Correction Officers can use their handcuffs 2 to 3 times daily to have to restrain a violent inmate and very few even go one week without having to deal with a very violent physical confrontation of some sort. Plus, Correction Officers are not dealing with law abiding citizens. They're dealing with the worst of the worst each and every day and the ratio can be as high as two officers for forty to fifty inmates at a time. And let's not forget Correction Officers are armed with only their physical abilities and mental capacity when dealing 100% of the time with the worst that society has to offer; murderers, rapist, pedophiles, kidnappers, robbers and drug dealers...

That being said, in no means do we minimize any Law Enforcement agency job so be it Police, D.E.A. (*Drug Enforcement Administration*), U.S. Marshals, I.C.E. (Immigration and Customs Enforcement), F.B.I. (Federal Bureau of Investigation) State Police, or for that matter even Fireman. All we're trying to do in this chapter is highlight and help people (even those who work in those other law Enforcement jobs) learn the tough work and expertise a Corrections Officer must have. All we're asking for is the respect we as Correction Officers have earned and we do give back much respect for our peers in Law Enforcement and the Firefighters.

Many times I've seen the look on the faces of Law Enforcement Officers who don't work in Corrections when they need to come into the jail for a tour or to interview a subject/inmate and hearing those doors slam shut behind them it's definitely an eye opener for most of them.

If anyone ever tells you they aren't concerned or a bit scared the very first time they walk into the jail or prison they're full of shit.

You see as a CO you are face to face with the worst society has to offer and you do so with your defense of hand to hand skills and a pair of handcuffs. It takes a special type of human being to walk the corridors and sit in a housing complex with knowing that's all you have and most of the time alone with anywhere from twenty to a hundred inmates or more at a time.

You have to have a great sense of your surroundings and be able to anticipate trouble. Preventing this trouble is not always possible in a jail, especially these days when the population of inmates are a good percentage of gang members who have very little respect or care for anyone's safety and are constantly in need of proving themselves to their fellow gang members.

Imagine being in the middle of a huge fight between two gang members or several from each gang for that matter, right in your work area and you're all alone, a situation nobody would want to be in. But to a CO it's a common occurrence and that's just part of the job.

It's common for a CO to have to get into the middle of a fight, getting brought into something like that is unfortunate because that's when injuries occur. Of course that's not the only way injuries occur, assaults on officers in the jail are high and unfortunately a common occurrence also and that's something we live with daily. It's nothing we complain about because that's our job, a job we take very seriously, and don't ask for much, except for some respect for the tough job we do.

More and more Correction Officers are collaborating with our brothers and sisters from many other Law Enforcement organizations doing specialty work, in the areas of gang units, warrants, D.E.A. investigations, Swat, Bomb units and hostage negotiations to name a just a few.

(above is a Highly Skilled Corrections Swat Team Training; teams like these are used for Riots, Cell Extractions and other emergencies that occur inside the facility.)

Corrections officers have become a highly trained group of individuals over the last twenty five years and now can stand toe to toe with our friends and peers in Law Enforcement. I believe, during this time we have started to earn more respect from our peers knowing that we have their backs and we are trusted and highly trained and capable Law Enforcement Officers able to perform Law Enforcement functions not only within a Corrections facility but also out on the street.

Long gone are the days where a Correction Officer would just grab a set of keys and walking the corridors of a jail facility, Corrections have taken on a new face and with that comes new responsibilities and earned respect. Training has been an integral part of the daily lives of many officers because that's what the public expects from us these days. Being professional and well trained are an essential part of our job and is most important. I can't stress enough about the mutual respect needed when all areas and departments of Law Enforcement work together.

I have just one or two more thoughts I would like to go over real quickly before we end this chapter. And I'd like to start off by asking you the reader a few questions. When you think of the Corrections Officer or more commonly you probably think of them as "Jail Guards"; what image of an individual comes to mind? Is it even close to anything that we've described up to this point so far? Do you truly see Corrections Officers as Law Enforcement Officers, peers on the same level as you would see a Police Officer on the street?

I'm willing to bet a large percentage of readers would fall into that category of seeing a Corrections Officer as that typical stereotype portrayed by Hollywood or truly not even having a clue of what we do and how we do it. And that's okay because it's no secret, every Corrections Officer knows how the general public feels about them and how his or her peers judge them. And yet we still perform as the professionals we are and that's just another notch in our belt that makes us who we are. It's also one of the main reasons why Joe and I are writing this book.

Now like I said, before I finish this chapter I want to leave you with one or two more thoughts. And it starts with another question. Think of one of the most dangerous places you have ever seen or heard of, like maybe the projects in a gang infested neighborhood or a dark alley in an inner-city street in a high crime area. I think you catch my drift here, RIGHT? Now here comes my question. Would you walk around those areas for eight straight hours every day, five days a week? Well guess what, the inside of all jails and or prisons is made up of 100% of those individuals that make those areas as dangerous as they are. That's what a Corrections Officer deals with on a daily basis. So you can take all of that Hollywood mumbo-jumbo and all of your preconceived concepts of what you think about a Corrections Officer is and throw them right out the window. And for all of you Police Officers who say hey I work those streets and neighborhoods every day. Well we're not taking any credit away from you we're smart enough to know it was you who brought them to us in the first place. All we want from you is the same recognition we give you.

Listen there's really no way I can truly explain here in this book to you what it's like to be inside those walls, behind those doors when they close and lock. It's just one of those feelings that you have to experience to believe and know. I guess one of the best ways I could try is by asking you if you were to go to prison tomorrow how do you think you would feel once you walked in, what type of emotions would you be feeling, how heighten would your senses be and what type of thoughts do you think would be racing through your mind? Well the Corrections Officer is no different; now you may say oh you're trained you're an officer that's your job and that's my point although we're still human as you, we are professionals and deal with that scenario every day we go to work.

All I'm trying to say here is unless you've walked a mile in a Correction Officers shoes you'll never know what these brave men and women deal with to ensure the care, custody and control, basically the protection to society from its worst nightmares. So I think… no I know, it's time that they're given the decency, respect and thanks that they so warrant and deserve not only from their counterparts in law-enforcement but also by the community at-large.

# CHAPTER 5

## Tools Of The Trade

Nothing has changed more in the last twenty five years in this profession as much as the tools we use to perform our jobs as Corrections Officers! And that is true for not only what we use inside the jail but as well as the tools we use outside the jail.

These tools we use in today's day and age while protecting and serving the community are and do play a very big role in not only officer safety but making the facility more secure. The general public would be surprised to know that many CO's are working the front lines with your local and federal law enforcement agencies side by side!

But that's not the way it was at one time, to start, years ago, when it all began for me, I was issued a badge and told to purchase a set of handcuffs which would be the only thing that I would have on my person to help me do my job, the tools of that time that a CO had to use would be only your own defensive skills and the guts you either had or better yet the pair of balls you'd better grow.

If you were attacked by a prisoner back then and even in some cases today, you would have to stare right at the situation, and get down and dirty with it. You see in our job there is no room for backing down or pushing it off on someone else. You have to stand your ground and let these inmates know who is running the facility and that means having the balls to do whatever it takes to protect your ass or stop an assault on another officer or an inmate. As a rookie if you're unaware of this fact, you will learn very fast that your peers will demand that you have and show courage in these situations and be able to hold your own and that you're someone who can be counted on.

It's easy for outside liberal agencies to criticize us for some of our actions. And that's because you'll never see them getting down and dirty and being assaulted verbally or physically by an inmate or as a matter of fact sadly even giving an officer who does on a daily basis the benefit of the doubt. They're more interested in standing up for the scumbags of the world that are incarcerated. Ironically many times we have to protect these people while they're in our facility lending their liberal sympathetic ears to the lies and stories that are told to them from those scumbags and they're buying every single word from them as if it was spoken by God. This is where one of our must valuable tools comes into effect "CAMERAS" because cameras don't lie and in most of these cases all we need to do is go to the camera for the real truth.

Well, as you can guess these (liberal) groups don't give us any respect and thus the reason they don't get that much respect back from us either. We do a very tough job and put our life on the line each day. So if we get no respect, we give NO RESPECT that's a code that Correction Officers live by whether it applies to inmates or these liberal organizations.

Over the years many effective tools and elite teams have been added to facilities throughout the country that can/do help in the running and making of a more secured and controlled environment within the facility. In this chapter as you probably already figured out, we will point out the most up-dated modern tools used to fight this ongoing "WAR" between Correction Officers and inmates. To not only help in maintaining the custody, care and control of the inmates but also to eliminate contraband in the form of, cell phones, drugs and weapons from coming into the facility. Contraband can also range from things as simple and seemingly not inherently dangerous like money to things that are extremely dangerous like weapons that are "homemade" like a razor blade that is melted into the end of a toothbrush handle or just a gun or knife that's smuggled into the jail or prison.

The use for contraband takes on many forms whether it's to increase an inmate's power or status within the facility or help by aiding in an escape plan or used for protection. Contraband can also take on a monetary value to buy things such as extra food or cigarettes or to pay for something they want done or even just used to commit a violent act.

Those scenarios occur in almost every jail and prison in the country. You have to remember that many inmates/prisoners are incarcerated not because they're stupid, it's because they committed a crime and many are ingenious. Which makes this "WAR" we fight to maintain control, a never ending battle and proves these new modern tools an invaluable asset.

The use of OC spray is probably the most widely used and a very effective method of squashing and minimizing the physical confrontations we have with violent inmates. Before we started using OC, a corrections officer had only one solution in stopping an aggressive violent inmate or an assault between two inmates and that was physical force and calling for back-up. The use of OC can come in different forms, sprayed from a canister and also shot from a weapon in a form of a ball, both are very effective and work most of the time. Yes there are some people that the spray does not affect and I've seen that happen on a few occasions. Using OC requires training and that includes that officers be requirement to get sprayed with OC. I'm telling you it's one of the worst feelings I've experienced. Getting sprayed was horrible, I had trouble breathing, excruciating pain in my eyes and couldn't open them, also burning in every area the OC touched! Once sprayed it become very easy to control the combative inmate and prevent the staff and the inmate from any further physical harm.

Another very important tool used in some but not all jails and prisons are the use of K-9 dogs. I can't tell you how much of an effective tool these beautiful animals are in preventing and controlling inmates during inmate movement and quashing disturbances. One K-9 Officer can do the work of ten officers when it comes to controlling a situation. These K-9 teams are assigned to work around-the-clock within the jail and believe me when I tell you they provide a very strong deterrent in the jail as well as out on the street assisting other law-enforcement agencies. Most Sheriff's Department utilize their canine teams inside and outside of the jail in the area of patrol, narcotics detection, accelerant detection, search and recovery and explosives detection.

When most people think of law-enforcement K-9 dogs that work inside Jails or Prisons. They think of a mean German Shepherd in an apprehension or attack mode getting ready to bite a "bad guy" or sniffing around looking for drugs or other contraband.

Well this quick little story I'm going to tell you is going to show the other side of this wonderfully unbelievable fine-tuned animal.

It was finally graduation day from the K-9 Academy. And I couldn't be more excited to start this new endeavor in my career with my partner Thor (A male German shepherd.) I had Thor since he was 10 weeks old and started preparing him for what I knew he would eventually have to go through in the K-9 Academy. And without bias I can truly say he excelled and was one of the finest dogs they had ever graduated from that Academy.

During graduation we put on a little show. The scenario was an inmate had just stabbed an officer and was fighting with another officer. We had an officer dress up in a bite suit and pretend to be attacking another officer.

Once Thor and I arrived, I immediately unhook the lead from his collar and commanded him to attack. So with the loud "GET HIM" from me,

Thor started running towards the officer who was playing the inmate. Once he was close enough he leaped into the air and delivered a bite so hard and vicious that it brought out the woo's in the crowd. I ran up to him commanded him to release and sit. Then the officer playing the inmate was handcuffed and escorted out of the room.

Once we were in the hallway the officer who was playing the inmate was taking off the bite suit. He looked at me and said "hey Tom he really got me good, he went right through the sleeve on the suit check this out." And as he lifted up his arm all I could see was blood.

One of the other officers who was there from our department but not from the canine unit said "you guys are crazy." Then he turned and looked at me and said "especially you Duncan, you have two small kids at home and you bring this dog into your house."

Well I looked at him and all I could do was laugh. And this is why, two weeks before graduation we had a snowstorm. My son Tommy who was just seven years old at the time wanted to go outside and play in the backyard with the dog. So my wife bundle him up in his snow suit and I let him and the dog outside in the back. Both my wife and I just sitting inside the house watching both of them running around going crazy in the snow, all we could do is sit there and laugh.

I got up to get another cup of coffee when I heard my wife calling me saying "Tom get back in here you have to see this." When I returned Tommy was standing outside crying and Thor had his glove in his mouth. Then Thor started backing up shaking his head and Tommy started running after him crying and screaming "give me back my glove Thor." They went on like that for about five minutes, then Tommy finally gave up and came back to the house.

Here is what people like that officer at graduation from my department don't understand about these dogs. That dog took the glove off my sons hand with his mouth and didn't put a mark on my kid. My kids could jump on that dog while he was eating, take bones away from him while he was chewing on them, fall and trip over him when he was sleeping. And that dog would just look at them like please leave me alone.

But you put that dog into a work scenario like the one at graduation or any other real life situations, and that dog looked like one of the most vicious dogs you ever saw.

That's the beauty of having a well-trained law-enforcement canine dog that performs at an unbelievable high level at work and once back at home falls into being that loving household pet… - *In memory of the best partner I ever had Thor 1993-2004*

Shakedowns are a vital tool used to search out and prevent inmates from getting or keeping contraband and using them, such as homemade shanks which can be used as weapons. No matter what systems are put in place contraband in many forms such as tobacco, illegal drugs, matches… etc seem to find their way into the facility! You may wonder how, but the biggest and most common way is lackluster work by some employees this will always be an issue and needs to be addressed immediately when discovered.

One of the most frightening things is that these shanks come in many forms and are easy to make with items that are commonly accessible to inmates such as toothbrushes sharpened at the ends to make a weapon, and pieces of metal found off bunks can also be made into knives. I've also seen a projectile made from a rubber band that could be easily shot at someone. Basically anything an inmate can find in their housing area can be made into a knife and used on another inmate and or staff.

(In Corrections there is NO ROOM for mistakes. So when your eyes are your best tools, they better be dam good; because it can be the difference between Life or Death. It's called CONSTANT VIGILANCES...)

Contraband in the form of drugs and alcohol can be a deadly combination when used with a weapon. Alcohol or as called by the inmate population "hooch" is made from taking fruit or juice that has a high sugar content and placing it in either a plastic bag or a cooler with bread and letting it sit to ferment for a couple of weeks. The bread acts as a yeast which turns the sugar into alcohol! This is something we always look for during our shakedowns.

Another valuable tool we use during these shakedowns are snake cameras that can look into drains, behind or in between tight places or even cracks in the wall. We also use mirrors to look under bunks and tables. To tell the truth there is nothing more effective than just using your hands when you "CAN" to feel and to look thru the entire area.

Many times one of the bests tool or tools that is used to prevent weapons and drugs from coming into or staying inside the facility is not a tangible tool but a mental tool and that is the correction officers ability to obtain a bond with certain inmates he feels can and will provide confidential information or so-called "rats" known among the ranks of the inmate population. Inmate informants are invaluable in our profession and provide us with information that we can and do use every day to combat the entering of illegal drugs and inmates making weapons.

During these shakedowns the entire housing area or cell is searched ending with the pat down search of the inmates. Remember these searches must be thorough and one officer not doing his or her job during these searches the right way can result in assaults and or death of within the inmate population or staff.

Listen, we've all worked with officers that sometimes fall short and do as little as possible like in any other profession but in ours it's our duty because it's our own personal safety that's being compromised. So after identifying these officers they must be addressed, even if it's done on a one on one basis.

Nobody in any profession wants to be labeled as a rat by their fellow coworkers but remember it's the person who's not doing his or her job that can get you killed. That's why it's so important that they be singled out and I've always felt that addressing it on a more personal level at first is helpful.

Also remember, we all enjoy having a good laugh at work and there are times we can and do. But when it's time to be serious and do our job, there is no room in this profession for slacking when our lives on the line.

# CHAPTER 6

## Hey Rookie Listen Up!

**W**ell who would we be to say no don't do it, or yeah it's a great job go for it. We can't even tell you to get as much information about the job first, before you leap into this career path, so you can try to make a decision if it's right for you; because there is nothing, not even this book that will prepare you for what it's like.

You can't take a college course and even a Corrections Academy won't prepare you 100% for what the job is like. The only thing that's going to give you a TRUE feel for what this job is like, is walking that walk on a daily basis for at least a year (and that's if you can even make it that long). But we can say this; it's a job that not everyone can do.

We wish there was a program that individuals could take to truly understand the nature of the beast that the Corrections Officer must take or work with on a daily basis. The mind games he must play, the abuse he must take, the feeling of always having to be vigilant on high alert of every second of every day while at work. The political games he must have to play in order to not be ostracized by the administration. The feeling like there's hundreds of people against you and you only have a few brothers that you can truly trust. The feeling that you have every morning at work that your main objective today as it was yesterday and every day before to go home safe, alive back to your family and for them to understand that despite all of this you come to this job every day.

We can't even tell you how many Thanksgivings, Christmases and Easter dinners were spent in the officer's dining room. Or how this job sticks with you long after you leave it each day and how you become less tolerant with people in just your everyday life because of the job. Just be aware of this, this job will affect your family and your friends outside of work. Now on to what degree, is undetermined and it varies from officer to officer. And we haven't even touched on how this job affects your mental health and all the physical issues that can occur with a lengthy career in corrections.

Listen we are not trying to scare anyone here out of becoming a Corrections Officer, after all we made a career out of it, with good money, great benefits. Now that we are retired. We have a great pension with great benefits and lots of fond memories and good times we shared with fellow coworkers. All we are trying to do is lay out as many facts as we can and let you know that there is really nothing that can prepare you to know whether you're fit for this job or not, other than doing this job.

(One of the first things a Correction Officer will learn is: that the look in an inmates/prisoners eyes can tell him a lot...)

We are often asked what it was like to be a Corrections Officer and what it takes to be one. One of our first answers is, you not only need to be mentally strong, you need to be able to handle yourself physically, be a good communicator and have great critical thinking skills. You must also have good self-control. Now this one, although it's not a must, it's a big PLUS; be and stay in good physical shape, being physically strong is a great asset, so working out in a gym should be an ongoing part of your life style. Working out really serves a dual purpose, it also helps to relieve anxiety and stress and most of all DON'T become complacent in how you work. A lot of Correction Officers like to think of themselves as glorified babysitters, this attitude can get you killed real fast.

Over the years in this profession we have seen many changes in the way things are done and the way the newer employees handle the job. Going way back to the day when we first started in Corrections. We (the Rookies or even Officers with less than five years on the job) came to work every day looking up to our supervisors for guidance and followed their words to a tee! There was an unwritten respect we had for our supervisors and the veteran officers that worked with us on our shifts.

Being a veteran back then you could feel the respect from the new officers and it gave them a sense of pride knowing they were passing their knowledge of the job on to us rookies! We remember listening to every word of advice coming from these guys and girls who truly had a wealth of knowledge that you can't read in any books and wasn't in our manuals and procedures and you couldn't even for some reason learn it in the academy. These officers just had the greatest teacher on their side... TIME.

Everything they taught us not always made sense at the time, but eventually it became clear when the situations aroused, there is something to be said about knowledge gained by experience and that's something that should always be respected in our field. The veteran officers have put in a ton of sweat and hard work that many of the younger officers take for granted. In many ways the job has become much easier because of these veteran officer who have put many hours of sweat into our field.

We would always tell rookie officers that the most important things they learn, are from the veterans who have lived through everything they will experience and plenty they will never have to because of them. So if you're just starting out in this crazy business remember one thing! You don't know JACK SHIT... That's why you should take these words to heart: always respect your fellow veteran officer and listen carefully to his or her words of wisdom.

The reason we felt so strongly to write about this "VETERAN ISSUE" was because all too often this new generation of officers can't even imagine let alone understand the great strides that have been accomplished in our field over the last thirty years. Technology today has and is playing a major role in the success we now enjoy in this career and many of these young officer take that for granted. Only a foolish man or a rookie wouldn't realize that, thus the importance to remember these veterans and pay them the <u>respect they deserve</u> because they're the ones who lived through this transition that made these changes and ideas possible.

Okay let me just make one thing clear, we are not trying to come down hard on every single rookie, there are a few wise ones out there. That do pay heed to what an older veteran has to say. But for the most part there are plenty of newer rookies that don't appreciate what has been done before them <u>and some</u> let me stress that again <u>and some</u> with attitude so bad that they just really don't even care. We just saw this gradually increasing before we left and that's why it's being addressed in this book, because we hope to make changes in a way a new rookie would perceive a veteran on the job.

Far too many times these newer guys are questioning the older veterans and they're not questioning them out of trying to gain a deeper or true understanding, it's out of sarcasm or an attitude that who are you to tell me what to do after all we're both officers. Many times we have heard responses like; why do I have to do that, who are you to give me orders, hey you do things your way, I do things my way, or Yeah Right, Okay Whatever... After a veteran gives a directive to a rookie officer. Those are just a few statements that Tom and I would have never even imagined saying to a veteran when we first started. Unfortunately like we stated before, this attitude, this paradigm, that these rookie officers are coming out of the academy with, is like a fast growing cancer and if left unchecked can have real devastating effects on their lives and careers. Sadly but true for a large percentage, they won't even realize this until they, and even if they last that long, become veterans themselves.

So hey rookies listen up again, for one last call out from two veterans on behalf of all the other veterans out there. You don't know SHIT and those old timers you're working with are filled with experience and knowledge that you can't even begin to understand. So take as much of it in as you can. Hopefully it will shape your career and turn you into a better officer and above all keep you safe and get you out of this profession alive and with a sound healthy mind.

Now I must also touch on a subject that some of my supervisor friends may not agree with or like. The hardest part of starting your supervisor career and one that I hope all of you get to experience is having to supervise and give orders to friends and coworkers that you have worked side by side with for years. It's something that we all faced when we were promoted and can be very easy if done with humility and common sense. Far too many times I've seen promotions get into the heads of a few and they don't know how to handle their success with humility.

Always remember the old saying, "remember where you came from!" No statement can be more truer! Remember as supervisors we not only have a tough job, but a very important one. One in which we have to make sure we keep the morale in the department positive. One thing that really bothered me and I had to address this with some supervisors, is when I've seen them yelling and disciplining officers in their command in front of other officers, and worst then that in front of inmates in the jail. When you do get promoted or already are, please don't fall into that trap of thinking you're more important than the officer and remember that was once you. Treat your officers the way you expected or wanted to be treated when you were an officer and you can't go wrong.

Now I do obviously know sometimes discipline is warranted, but the way you handle it is key and can be the difference of making sure that never happens again. Make it as positive as possible. I know it's hard because there are times you will be tested by your officers and inmates but handle it professionally and firm and you'll get their respect.

I had an old supervisor who wasn't really liked by many of the officers and he really didn't care, even worse he wasn't respected (in my opinion even means more) and here's just one reason why. During a routine shakedown of a cell the address and wife's name of an officer was found under an inmate's bunk and this said inmate had been involved in an assault of this officer in the past and there was an ongoing court case. Well somehow, the court released these papers to the inmate during discovery and it had this personal information about the officer on it and it was not blacked out by the court the way it should have been.

So you can just imagine the concerns that the officers had when they found this paperwork so they seized it immediately. The judge was notified of the mistake and ordered that the documents remain seized until the name and address were blacked out, then returned back to the inmate. Well this supervisor was advised of the judge's new order, but still refused and sent the paperwork back to the inmate. The supervisor justifying in his own mind that, that was the way the inmate got the paperwork from the court, so he should be allowed to keep the paperwork from the court.

Well as you can imagine I along with the officer who was the victim in this case became very angry with the actions of this supervisor. As you can also imagine when we confronted this supervisor and questioned him about his actions, the officer involved needed to be physically restrained by myself from causing this supervisor physical harm because of his lack of concern and disregard for the officers and his family's safety.

Now hopefully you're asking yourself the same question we ask ourselves as we left that conversation. Why in the hell would a supervisor do something like that? Something that could possibly harm this officer and his family. Still to this day I could not come up with an answer for that. All I can tell you is this type of stuff does happen.

I was eventually forced into calling the judge back and telling him what had just happened. The judge in return, furiously called this supervisor immediately and informed him that it would be in his best interest to heed the order previously given by the court to blackout said information. Long story short the matter was finally resolved as per the order of the court.

I tell this story because I want everyone to realize as Correction Officers we face many dangers from inmates but a lot of people don't realize we also face dangers from supervisors who have gotten too big for their own good in their mind and make poor decisions which can place us in an equal amount of danger or greater.

Moral of the story don't become that supervisor remember the safety of all your officers fall into your hands and that's a great responsibility. Please take this advice as serious as you can at all times.

The even sadder thing about this story is it's just one of many stories I can tell that highlights the fact that there are supervisors out there that just don't care and used poor judgment with no common sense when it comes to their officers or the security of the facility and this is one thing that can't continue to happen.

Bottom line: Never put anyone at risk at your facility! Safety first always! First the Officers then the Inmates...

# CHAPTER 7

## *Many Faces Of A Corrections Officer*

Throughout the many years I've spent working as a Corrections Officer, I've come to know many officers and one thing is for sure their countless individual personalities range differently like night and day.

One of the first that comes to mind and also one of my favorites is known as "The Topper." Yes, that's your fellow employee who thinks he or she is above all their peers and every time you have a story to tell or even every time you buy something. He or she has something bigger or better and always has a better story to tell. They're also someone who is totally ignorant of the fact that they have been talked about and laughed about for years by their peers for the bullshit artist that they really are.

And in this career we've also been blessed with the individual who is convinced that everyone in the administration is out to get them and has many theories on how and why. In my experience these officers never contribute to anything that is good or positive. They sow only descent and spread rumors that can spread like a cancer throughout the entire agency. The ironic thing about this type of personality is that, this person most of the time wants things handed to them, and never really wants to work hard or put forth the extra effort it takes to advance or make themselves a better officer. My best advice and as I have always try to do myself is to stay clear from this type of individual. The paranoia that fuels this individuals mind set is not only self-destructive but makes him one of the most unproductive officers there are. The fear that fills his mind with all those conspiracy theories he has, leaves no room for the true thoughts that should constantly be running through a Corrections Officers mind while at work.

That now brings me to the individual, and even worst of all who is the Supervisor, every time that there is a decision to be made, they are always looking to defer or call someone else to make that decision for them. Whether it be out of fear or insecurity in their own ability to make the proper decision. I've seen people make this mistake more times than I'd like to remember.

The approach that I've always tried to utilize and pass along to every employee, especially the supervisors who worked under me and who are counted on to make important decisions. Is to always make a firm decision and a swift one based on their experience and or gut feeling. My theory behind that is in making your own decision even if it's not the correct one, it's always more productive than someone else who looks to others to make them for them, because at least if you make a mistake it can become a learning experience. But the only way that can happen is by actually making a decision to begin with. In this line of work there's nothing worse than a shift commander or an officer not making a decision and waiting for or wanting someone else to make that important decision for them.

The next individual is the Lazy Officer: this is the officer whose just there to collect his paycheck and who only wants to do the minimum required amount of work. This officer can always be found looking for shortcuts. This is the officer who never fully reaches his or her true potential. I've seen it time and time again, this is the officer who is also using poor judgment and not only compromising the integrity and security of the facility and putting themselves and other officers in dangers way, because of their lack of vigilance. I've told many officers not to fall into this trap because it's very tempting sometimes to take shortcuts, remember it's the weakest link in the chain that compromises the safety of all the officers.

If I could somehow tattoo one saying on every new rookie's brain it would be work smart, do things the right way and remember getting home safe from your shift is your main concern. I've seen too many officers get hurt and lose their careers because of other officers' inattentiveness and lack of concern on the job. These officers should do everyone a BIG favor and find another profession, there is NO room for this in corrections.

The lazy officer is also the officer who rarely is ever successful in being promoted. In my experience the officers that work harder and seeks out or volunteers to be trained in all aspects of how the facility operates always seems to score higher on promotional tests and turns out to make a much better supervisor. This lazy officer is also the biggest crybaby after they have been disciplined, always running to their union representatives blaming everyone and everything except themselves and expecting their union representatives to go to bat for them. When they actually know deep down inside they haven't been doing their job correctly for a long time. When they lose their grievance process, they blame there union representatives for not fighting hard enough for them, it's the nature of the beast. This lazy officer never accepts responsibility and or seeing himself as the problem.

As a union representative for many years I've always believed in and fought for every officer who has ever brought a grievance in front of me, about a discipline action against him or any other factor. Fighting for officers rights as a union representative is a full-time job. But when an officers is wrong, the bottom line is the officer is just wrong, and there's nothing no representative can ever do about that. So if I could go back and just add to that tattoo on that rookie's brain. I would add this; don't be part of the problem and turn into an officer like this, the safety and well-being of everyone in your facility is counting on you.

The RAT, The BACKSTABBER or the ASS KISSER; whatever you want to call this individual, and almost every profession has at least one. Well in corrections we have them also, lurking around waiting to make a move that will make them look good and not caring who they throw under the bus whether it's true or not. These individuals in my mind are the most detrimental and shameful as you can get in life! Now you should know that when we say rat, it's not someone telling stories that are true, like a mob guy in the movies just out to save his own ass, the so called RATS in our profession tell lies to get ahead.

These people will do ANYTHING they can to get ahead and I mean anything. They lie, make up stories and even have gone as far as to bring contraband into the facility, only to find it themselves to try and look like the hero. Finding (just to name a few) things like knives, drugs, cell phones and keys; when in fact they actually brought them in themselves!

How about an officer who writes anonymous letters to his boss bad mouthing another officer just because he wants his job! Well it's been done, and everyone can pretty much figure out who wrote the letter. It doesn't stop just at the officer level, how about the brass, jealous of his or hers other brass (Brass is another name for a supervisor) to undermine them just to make them look bad. These people would also have a reputation of being a rat!

What's unfortunate is society has rules or for that matter decent people have morals and ethics in which they live by, because the most easiest way in dealing with individuals like this, would be by taking them for a nice little walk with a few of the good old boys into a nice dark place. I have a funny feeling that would put an END to this individual's lowlife tactics. But unfortunately that little voice inside our head that decent people have, stops us from doing things like that, and besides who would want to lose their pension or your job over a RAT.

Believe me these people are few and far between, but I'm willing to bet every profession has them and there's no other person from the rookie line officer all the way to a top admin supervisor that hates to have to deal with individuals like this in our profession, these RAT officers are just plain despicable.

And what makes this even more despicable is the fact that some administrations condoned this and use it as a tool to benefit themselves. I've seen it far too many times, like allowing these RATS to enter into their so-called inner circle of trust within the senior administrators' level. It's when cronyism like this is allowed to flourish within a department and people are moved up the chain of command based on the lies they tell, and the way they're used by the administration to hurt other officers who have targets on their back. This will always hurt and destroy a department's morale. I've seen firsthand an administration take an individual, such as this and place them in a position of authority over an officer or supervisor that has earned his or her own rank, just so the admin can have control over certain individuals.

That's why we as professionals will always push for seniority to be a major factor in all promotions and the use of civil service tests. If I had my way all these RATS would be identified with the tattoo right across their foreheads and left to fend for themselves.

This next officer, as hard as it is to admit it is the type of officer who everyone looks at and says: "how the hell did he or she ever make it this far in life or for that matter even make it through the Academy." Now don't get me wrong this officer may have a great personality, be well liked by everyone and even have your back in a situation where you need him. But the one trait about him that shines the brightest, it's his inability to function at a level which is required and expected from a Corrections Officer. Another words he's as dumb as a rock, he doesn't have a clue and his ability to be able to learn from others just doesn't seem to be able to sink in.

This type of officer is usually the most prone to being manipulated and used by the inmate population for their betterment. Unfortunately, he's also the type of officer which puts everyone else at high risk. I guess every profession in the world has there individuals who slipped in through the cracks, kind of scary though when you think about it on the law-enforcement level. Well fortunate enough for the rest of us in corrections I can truly say throughout my career I've only truly encountered maybe a handful of these individuals, but then again in this case one is one too many.

Then of course you have the officer who truly depicts what a professional Corrections Officer is/should be. Hard-working, knows their job well and is constantly vigilant, this officer is consistent with the way they work, is firm but fair with the inmates and who has proven time and time again, that GOOD officers will and always will, have his fellow officer's backs.

This is the officer every recruit while in the academy aspires to be. Now, where, how and when it changes for some officer, the reasons are unknown.

Last but not least is the most important officer of all. The officer who has given his/her life in the line of duty.

Every single day Hundreds of Thousands of Correctional Officers throughout this country put their lives on the line to serve the public and greater good. And every year the number of these brave officers killed in the line of duty goes up.

Now the death of no Law-Enforcement officer is ever easy to handle (Police or Correctional) and unfortunately occurs way too often. The law-enforcement family is a tightly woven brotherhood and the pain or our fallen heroes affect us forever (our BLUE LINE runs deep.)

But what the general public doesn't know, is that 90% of the time the manner and facts in which a Correctional Officer is killed when in the line of duty is hidden from them. Now this cannot be said about our counterpart the Police Officer, because they're killed while out in public. Whereas the Correctional Officer is attacked and killed behind closed walls; thus limited information concerning the death can be released and some of it can be concealed. The factors for this can range from (Good to Bad) like wanting to protect the family in not letting the general public know all the details to wanting to protect the facilities name.

One of the first things the general public should/needs to know is that a high percentage of all Correctional Officers killed in the line of duty, are killed in the most horrific, inhuman cruel ways imaginable.

Without getting into too much detail, can you imagine what would happen to a female officer during a riot while being held hostage? And if you don't think the same happens to a male officer then you're sadly mistaken.

Raping a female officer during a hostage situation can be done solely for the pleasure of the inmates/prisoners. Whereas the rape of a male officer is done to punish him and most often is substituted from a physical rape to an object rape. Unfortunately these rapes can last for hours and even days in most cases violent beatings accompany these rapes which are brutal and sometimes in themselves are the cause of death. And don't think that the officers who are not raped are getting off easy. Many are physically tortured: stabbed with shanks in the hands and feet, then the arms and legs, then cut around the genitalia until they bleed to death, how about being poked in the eye with a pencil and having it push all the way into your brain, or being burned all over your body before being lit on fire, or how about being drowned by having bleach poured down your throat. Those are just some of the ways Correctional Officers have been killed over the years throughout correctional facilities in this country.

One thing is for sure, the killing of a Correctional Officer is seldom ever fast like it is with a Police Officer who is shot. Most of the time Correctional Officers are killed in ways no one wants to hear about.

One thing everyone should keep in mind is Correctional Officers goes to work every day knowing in their minds that all of that and more is a possibility and can happen to them on any given day.

These unsung heroes who give their lives protecting society from their worst nightmares deserve to NEVER be forgotten. And the unsung heroes who are still working behind the walls deserve recognized and respected for the job they do.

**Taking Care of Our Own**: The C.P.O. Foundation

The Correctional Peace Officers Foundation is an organization out to help surviving families of fallen Correctional Officers killed in the line of duty. The C.P.O. Foundation is a national, non-profit charitable organization <u>NOT</u> affiliated with any political organization and or groups or committees of any kind.

We would highly recommend all Correctional Officers to check out the C.P.O. Foundation. Information on membership and membership benefits can be found on their Website: <u>WWW.CPOF.ORG</u>
Correctional Peace Officers Foundation
P.O. Box 348390
Sacramento, CA 95834-8390
Phone: 916.928.0061 or 800.800.CPOF (2763) Fax: 916.928.4796
Email: <u>mail@cpof.org</u>

<u>May GOD BLESS all of our brother and sister who were killed in the line of duty, for they truly are FALLEN HEROES.</u>

# CHAPTER 8

## Bad Things Can And Will Happen

Throughout your career you will find out that many things will and can go wrong during the course of your shift, and what you do to prevent these situations is very important because it can end a potential crisis or exacerbate it, thus turning it into a major crisis!

Dealing with problem inmates, mentally challenged inmates, gang members, inmates who have committed horrendous crimes and inmates who are manipulative towards staff are an everyday hurdle every jail/prison staff will encounter, that's a given in this line of work. But the biggest change today are the amount of mentally challenged inmates that are being arrested and probably belong in a hospital not jails or prisons that are not equipped to properly handle them. One of the biggest problems with this is many of them for whatever the reason, neglect or are just misdiagnosis by so called qualified mental health staff within the facility go without their psych medication and cause havoc for staff every day. Dealing with this type of inmate requires special training and patience that can only be divulged over time. Thus classification and being aware of who these inmates/prisoners are, is crucial when housing them. Without that, many of them begin to be bullied by other inmates and it's our job to be aware of it as soon as possible when this occurs and reporting it so proper action can be taken. If this is not addressed correctly and expeditiously and is allowed to flourish inside the jail/prison this will result in many problems ranging from simple fights, rapes, the stealing of the inmates food to major physical assaults on inmates simply because they cannot defend themselves due to a medical condition. Which is why, getting back to my original point these inmates need to be properly identified, given proper medication and segregated from general population. That's why in the jail I worked at and I'm sure many others there are designated areas where challenged inmates will be housed under a 24/7 (24/7 is a term used that means twenty four hours a day seven days a week) watch by the corrections staff. This is most valuable during the classification process while working together with the medical staff so a more accurate placement of the inmate can be made to suit his needs. I've seen many officers dealing incorrectly with these mentally challenged inmates, causing assaults not only on themselves but also on other staff.

Until the Government and the medical community come up with a plan and some solutions for this population of inmate, we will continue to struggle and find ways to make life in the jail/prison more manageable for them and most importantly to insure the safety of the Correction Officers and civilian staff working inside the facility.

Manipulative inmates can and are very dangerous and they're in every jail and prison across this country and can be like a cancer in a facility and many times their little mind games and plans result in very bad things happening. A weak minded officer or a stupid rookie that are used by this type of inmate can be bribed into doing things that are against your agency rules and regulations and are even criminal in nature.

Many officers often face disciplinary action and even arrest for succumbing to the pressure placed on them by this type of inmate/ prisoner and it all starts with what I like to call the little hook. Which is getting an officer to break a small rule at first and it grows bigger and bigger each time. I wish I had a dollar for every officer I told to not ever let yourself fall into this trap, your career and family depends on you and nothing ever good comes from this encounter.

The best way to make sure you don't fall into this trap is by dealing with this type of inmate in a straight forward way. Report any type of manipulating he may try, to your superior officer, and by also being tough enough to even report another officer, you see or feel is falling in a trap. Remember not all staff are concerned about this as we good ones are and unfortunately, a lot end up on the wrong side because of their bad choices.

Years ago an inmate was in our facility who fit this role to a tee. He bragged about being connected to certain "underworld individuals" and he was. He also promised many things to many people. He was a " true mafia RAT" in every sense of the word and his constant search for a weak link in the chain of great officers continued every day until he found pay dirt with a weak officer who was promised a mere $100,000 dollars for his help in aiding in an escape plan with this inmate from the facility. And one night sure enough this weak minded officer walked this inmate right out of the jail, with the help of the inmates' attorney who brought in civilian clothes during a visit. Which by the way all three carefully planned out, that's how bad this officer was hooked.

Sadly not all officers are lawful and can be trusted and that goes for attorneys as well. The one thing that could have blown this whole plan to hell would have been diligent work by the staff, it could have prevented this escape, but unfortunately at times facilities (which translates into Officers) can be lax at, so we must not only know that, we need to be on our toes and trust no one when it comes to security. We must constantly look for the unexpected and expect it.

So this inmate in fact did escape and by the time the staff was alerted to it, it was way too late. The plot eventually was uncovered (as they always are) by the authorities who investigated it and the officer was shamed, his life was ruined. He lost everything, marriage, friends and of course was arrested and spent time in jail himself.

The reenactment was eventually aired on Americas Most Wanted and was an embarrassment to all of us as a department, and personally a hatred towards this officer who took our trust for granted was felt by everyone. Good news is the officer rightfully spent time in jail for his criminal act and the "RAT" was eventually caught.

Also, during the investigation it was discovered that a few other officers were on the hook although not having knowledge of the escape plot they did do a few favors inside the faculty for the "RAT" inmate and were also disciplined. This event as bad as it was, did do some good. It brought a new and tighter security of directives that was implemented, that if we had in place before this escape, would have prevented this from occurring.

Part of everyone's job each day should be to take a good look at your own facility, and ask yourself where the weak links are. I know it's a constant pursuit as an administration to locate the weak areas in our facility and address them immediately. This however was not done efficiently enough at the time and this is what occur.

One of if not the worst things, that can happen in a facility, as you all should be aware of, is an escape. If you are fortunate in your career this will never occur on your shift or at your faculty at all. I've been fortunate to not have this happen on any shift I've ever worked. No feeling is worse than to be working on the shift that this occurs on. But I feel the pain of it happening in my department.

A few things that can aid in helping an inmate escape range from dishonest, and weak employees who get trapped and make bad decisions to officers who are just plan lazy and get into a daily routine or rut and are not as vigilant in their responsibilities and take a short shrift approach during their shift. Taking shortcuts day after day, while they may not turn out bad for you one day, they can be disastrous the next. I would be very hesitant to advise taking any shortcuts no matter who is giving the order. As we all know administrators love to have us rush to get things done, but when something goes wrong who's holding the bag? YOU!

Be professional everyday regardless and take pride in your work and nobody should ever ask you to do something that will jeopardize your livelihood. I've see other escapes occur and in every case the main component is clear, the officer was either lazy or not as observant as he or she should have been. Remember your career and even your life can end abruptly one day based on the choices you make that day.

Here is a story about an inmate who committed a horrendous crime. I'd like to first start off by saying this story didn't happen at my facility and I wasn't a part of it, it's a story I heard. As a matter of fact it's a story I heard from another Corrections Officer that worked at a different facility than me, cough... cough... cough...

It starts off with the local police department that arrested this lowlife scumbag pedophile who they actually caught him on top of and in the act of sodomizing a six month old baby female corpse. Who he had previously kidnapped a few days prior to that date. Needless to say when the officers broke into the room and tried to arrest him, he resisted arrest, cough… cough… cough… and that resulted in this piece of shit getting multiple lacerations, broken ribs and a broken jaw, by the arresting officers.

Well once he was cleared by the hospital and brought to the jail everyone in the facility wanted a piece of this guy and I'm talking inmates and officers. Well one night on the midnight shift Sgt. (Let's call him) Graham-cracker notice that this inmates bandages were bled through with his blood. So he called together a group of very specially trained officers to help him determine what if any medical attention this said inmate may need. The bandages that were soaked with blood were on the inmates back so the Sgt. order the officers to remove the bandages and all involved came to the conclusion that the wounds that now were partly scabbed over were infected and needed to be treated, because after all an inmates health is one of our top priorities.

So the inmate was held down and bleach was poured on his back and the wounds were disinfected with a deck brush, and after about five or ten minutes of making sure all of the wounds were clean and free of any germs that may have cause this inmate problems he was re-bandaged, and placed (Thrown) back into his cell.

Now some liberals today may view that as cruel and unusual punishment, and some conservatives may see that as poetic justice, but I… personally view this story that I heard, cough… cough… cough… as Corrections Officers just doing their jobs. In making sure that, that inmate received the best medical care possible and if I wasn't mistaken that wasn't the only treatment he needed to help disinfect his wounds.

Now that's what I call old-school corrections right there for ya. I don't know how many newer officers nowadays even get a chance to help an inmate out like that which in my view is sad.

Every once in a while you'll get an inmate that comes into the facility who feels he needs to prove that he is a badass and won't take no shit from anyone. But he doesn't necessarily want to prove this by standing up to another inmates. So he says or does something to an officer trying to prove that he's a badass and won't take no shit from anyone (A.K.A. Dealing with a problem inmate.) FYI- This story happen while I was working in the jail down in Florida.

Well one morning while feeding breakfast I had an encounter which such an inmate. Now I should tell you this was while I was working a maximum-security floor in the jail. Now my feeding trustees that I handpicked and used every day to feed breakfast were two of the biggest guys on that floor and they had the worst street reputations as bad-asses and everyone on that floor knew them and knew about them.

Let's just say I rarely ever had any problems while feeding breakfast. I always paid my trustees well, with extra trays and also instructed them to never EVER handout a food tray that didn't have everything it was supposed to have on it.

So now this NEW inmate who wants to prove himself, is served his breakfast tray and immediately starts to bitch and complain to me about it. I tell him to shut up, sit down, and eat his tray of food and if he doesn't like it, throw it in the trash. I don't really care.

With that he stands up takes his tray of food throws it on the floor and tells me to go fuck myself I'm not eating that shit and I'm not cleaning that up. I respond by telling him you're going to clean that up or you're going to be sorry. He responded back by saying fuck-you! You can't make me clean up shit. I then again responded back to him by saying, listen you made that mess it's only fair that you clean it up and this is your last chance and opportunity to do so, I'm trying to be fair with you.

He responded back by saying fuck you. I then said okay if that's the way you want it that's the way you'll get it. After I was done feeding and the inmates were finished eating everyone was locked back into their cells and the mess still remained on the floor in the middle of the dayroom.

Now here is an example of a technique that can be used and is very effective in getting a point across to this type of inmate and all the others. That you're the wrong officer to try and prove your point to other inmates that you're a badass.

After everyone was locked in their cells. I pulled my two trustees back into the day room, and may I add in a decibel level to make sure that everyone could hear especially this inmate who was trying to prove a point. I said to my trustees: "both of you are not only going to clean this mess up you going to strip this floor and wax it, then buff it out and I don't care if it takes the whole shift to do it."

Well right after I said this, this inmate starts yelling out from his cell ok, ok, ok, C.O. I'll clean up the mess. I turned and looked at him and said too late, you had your opportunity, did you already forget you're a badass and you don't take no shit.

Well it took my trustees three hours to clean up the mess, strip the floor and wax it and I instructed them that if we ever have a problem like this again neither one of them would be a trustee ever again.

Well the next day when I returned to work that inmate that was trying to prove a point was in the infirmary, apparently he fell and slipped on a bar of soap. Again that's what I call "Old School Corrections at work"...

This next-story you're about to read I should warn you, it's truly disgusting. The only reason why I'm telling it is because when Joe and I decided to write this book we both concurred that no story should be omitted or left out simply based on the content. We felt it was important that if we were to tell a story on what truly happens behind the bars of the correctional facility and for our readers to get a true understanding of "Life as a Jailer" no story should be off-limits.

With that said here it goes; One part of the Correction Officers job which happens way too often is having to physically and forcefully extract a violent or mentally disturbed inmate from his cell. Now for the most part, most of these extractions occur under normal conditions and what I mean by that is there are no obstacles, special factors or conditions that need to be addressed when preforming basic cell extraction tactics.

For instants in some cases inmates may sprinkle baby powder or rub baby oil on the floor to make the conditions hazardous because then the floor becomes extremely slippery and gives the inmate a definite advantage. One technique to combat this condition is to throw down mattress once you enter the cell that officers can safely walk on. Another obstacle an inmate may try to employ is covering his entire body in baby oil thus making it extremely difficult to restrain him and secure him. I've even seen an inmate wrap himself up in toilet paper and threatening to lite himself on fire once we entered the cell, and as difficult as these situations are to deal with, there are many more so called tricks these inmates use.

But the one every corrections officer hates dealing with the most (and I'm not even coming close to trying to call this a trick) is the inmate that spreads his feces all over his cell and all over himself and starts throwing it at the officers as they enter the cell. Believe me when I tell you this, even though you're covered in special clothing this is and always will be the hardest and most difficult and disturbing cell extractions to deal with.

Okay this is where the story becomes really disgusting and remember I did warn you. I've had an inmate take his feces mix it up with smoking tobacco, place it in his mouth so that once the officers secured him and removed either face shields or helmets thinking it's safe, he would spit it into their faces. Now that was as I stated one of the most difficult cell extractions a Corrections Officer needs to deal with. Can you guess what would come in a close second? How about the inmate who has cups full of urine to throw at us and let's not forget the more dangerous side. The inmate who standing in a cell with a weapon like a jailhouse shank.

Cell Extractions! Just one of the many fun things that Correction Officers get to deal with on a daily basis at work.

Here's a story about an incident I mentioned earlier in the book but never elaborated on.

While working the jail one day down in Florida a 10-94 call went out. All officers respond, officer needs assistance! You can just imagine when a call like that goes out the whole jail becomes a madhouse, almost every officer start running and coming from every direction.

Well in this instance I was the first officer to respond to and find a fellow officer, a close friend of mine fighting with an inmate. Now in the Corrections Academy they like to teach you all these special techniques for subduing and securing a violent inmate. But they also teach you that sometimes in a fight these techniques can be difficult to apply and they like to stress one of the most important major facts while trying to overcome and secure the inmate, is hand placement. No matter how stressful or involved you become in a confrontation, it's very important to make sure you keep your hands and any other body part away from an inmate's mouth...

Now unfortunately this officer got so tangled up with this inmate that his right hand accidentally slipped up into the inmates face. That's when the inmate bit off his right index finger at the second knuckle and just as I was arriving at the scene the inmate spit it out on the floor.

Well needless to say that inmate ended up in the hospital with many severe injuries. The officer's finger was wrapped in ice and he was also transported to the hospital, an attempt to sow the finger back on was unsuccessful. The officer not only sub-stained a severe physical disability, the mental trauma also affected him so badly that he couldn't return back to work and was forced to retire under medical conditions.

I couldn't even count the number of times in my career that I had to fight an inmate while watching him snap at me like some wild animal trying to bite and kill its prey. And I'm sure that every Corrections Officer who is reading this right now can relate to what I'm saying. All too often in our line of work, situations like this arise and turn out to be just another day at the office for a Correction Officers...

Now the next type of inmate I'd like to discuss is the gang member that has infiltrated every jail and prison in the country and pose a very big threat to the staff. But in most cases the threats are directed toward other inmates.

Twenty five years ago there were only a handful of gang members in our correctional facilities. But today there are many more and in every nationality and race. This can be, and is, a classification nightmare for the staff, but there are a few ways this is done. After identifying the gang members and I hope your facility has a gang unit that specializes in this, the classification department has to decide what will be the facilities approach.

Will they place all the same gang members together or split them up, integrating them throughout the facility. Well at first, years ago that worked. Most facilities just spread them around so that one gang couldn't be strong enough to dominate areas of the jail. This has proven to be tougher today because the major gangs have way too many inmates recruited so the approach I've seen lately is to keep like gang members together.

This can cause additional problems to the staff when an inmate from that gang has to be reclassified for some reason and he or she cannot be placed in areas where rival gang members will definitely harm him. Gang dorm fights can range from just an old fashioned beat down on any inmate or inmates, too even another gang members for various reasons. The gang members will tell you, being a so called rat and not following orders from the gang leaders are the most common. I've seen assaults on gang members in both these cases.

Gang intelligence is crucial in our line of work and we would be helpless without the cooperation of many inmates who give us information. I've seen gang members throw scalding hot water on another inmates causing sever burning.

Remember anything that an inmate does to another inmate, like assaults can be turned around and also done to you if you're not on your "A" game that day. So remaining professional and fair but firm will in most instances keep the peace between the inmates and the staff, but as we all know that's not always the case.

With the newest technology being used now in most facilities, most areas are under constant video surveillance that is being recorded and the inmates know that. This has helped in the prevention of assaults somewhat and has helped in charging offenders of crimes in the institution which is also a deterrent.

Now the stories we can tell are endless, but I can guarantee one thing for sure, every story we tell in this book every C.O. in the country will most likely be able to say, "I've had that same situation at my jail or prison!" Just because of one simple fact, problem inmates are found in every facility.

Inmates who light themselves on fire, mentally ill inmates, inmates who have weapons and will not hesitate to use them, inmates who will bite you, gang inmates, inmates trying to manipulate you, inmates that are looking and planning an escape, inmates who want to fight you just so they can look tough in front of other inmates, inmates who place feces all over their bodies. I've had a female inmate in S.D.U. (*Segregated or Special Detention Unit A.K.A. "The Hole"*) take her own feces and write her name all over the cell walls where she was housed just because she thought it was funny!

How about the inmate who wanted to take feces, roll it up into a ball and start to throw it at us as we opened the cell door or even throw urine. There are so many bad things we can go into that happen to Correction Officers; how about the inmate who decides he or she wants to spit at an officer knowing they have AIDS... Like I said the stories are endless and every Corrections Officer knows them all too well, the only thing that changes are the names…

Until a few years back this type of behavior wasn't even a crime. But in today's day and age it's an aggravated assault and rightfully so! Throwing bodily fluids at Corrections Officers is an everyday occurrence at jails and prisons across this country. Oh and here's a question for you; where's the A.C.L.U. (American Civil Liberties Union)? I'll tell you where they are, they're more interested in standing up for an inmate's rights rather than standing up for the rights of the Corrections Officer who has to endure this. Try spraying this type of animal that's throwing this stuff at you with O.C. spray (A.K.A. *Pepper spray*, from "oleoresin capsicum") and see how fast the A.C.L.U. will come running to defend this animal and try to turn the table of justice on us! I've seen it over and over again.

Ask yourselves this question. What would you do if someone spit in your face? Well a Corrections Officer has to endure this behavior and has to do it professionally, and yes we have to get physical at times and that because there are no other alternative. And YES, we did pick this line of work to get into and by no means are we complaining about it, all we're asking for is the right support while we do our job.

Most people who have never worked in this crazy, stressful environment cannot even start to comprehend the lengths of restraint we (Correction Officers) must exhibit on a daily basis while at work! Nobody on the streets would ever even tolerate this, let alone having to act professional while dealing with it!

Dealing with the all these "Monday Morning Quarterbacks" is the biggest joke of all. They expect you to do nothing in the face of assaults upon us and inmates throwing bodily fluids at us. We are human beings also, and yes it's our job but who took this job expecting to have feces thrown at them, and when you do respond appropriately, you have an outside entity there waiting to come down on you, waiting for you to make a mistake so they can pounce on you, like the A.C.L.U. ! I'd love to say to all of them, get lost, we know what we are doing! We're the professionals! You have NO CLUE what really goes on.

We realize every profession has people who do things wrong for one reason or another, but these liberal organizations and also the people who believe these inmates/prisoners 100% all of the time. Need to really start listening to us Correction Officers, and realize we have one of, if not the toughest, most dangerous job in the country! And 99.9 % of the time we're justified in doing what we do.

# CHAPTER 9

## *Back in the Day...*

**W**ell "Back in the Day" the facility Tom and I worked at was known for being one of the toughest jails in the Country, and we certainly earned every bit of that reputation! The first thing you saw when you entered was a sign that read, "Welcome to the County Jail, this is not a country club!"

Back then it wasn't uncommon for many facilities throughout the state of New Jersey and even from outside of the state to request that we house an inmate because they couldn't handle them and every time our sheriff received such a request he didn't hesitate to grant it. Every time one of these so called tough guys, high risk or violent inmates was scheduled to arrive he was greeted by some of the toughest guys we've ever had the pleasure of working with.

Needless to say a high percentage of the times we had to wrestle around (or should I say kick the shit out of) a few of these so-called tough guys and 90% of the time they initiated it, those other 10%... well we just did that to let them know and make sure that they knew who was/is in charge of our facility.

As you all know a Corrections Officer can never afford to lose a fight, it's never an option. At our facility we had a post known as the "Hall Man" every shift the commanding officer would assign 4 to 5 officers as hall man. Where they would roam around mainly the first floor of the jail ready to respond to any and all incidents or assaults against an officer. They were also involved in booking and receiving new inmates. Many times when a new inmate thought that he would try and test the facility the other inmates who knew better would always start to whisper, man you really fucked up now, when they saw our crew on the way.

Now remember many times we had to respond to these incidences not even knowing what was waiting around the corner for us and with no weapons back then, not like many officers choose to use today. A lot of these new officers today when they hear the old-timers tell stories wish that they had worked back in a day where we could actually physically fight these inmates without the use of pepper spray, tasers, etc... Like they use today, we only had to rely on our fists and street-smarts to get the job done and always of course your fellow officers too.

Those were the so-called good old days when Corrections Officers could kick the shit out of inmates to keep them in line and even the inmates back then were tougher. They never went running to their mommies or calling their lawyers crying. That's because that was just the way things were done back then and everyone knew it.

But I have to confess, even though that was a lot of fun and Corrections Officers gained the respect of the inmates the hard way. In today's day and age it is a lot safer for the staff, with the tools we now have available. Officers can work a lot smarter which makes it a lot safer.

In this chapter "Back in the Day" we're (Tom & I) going to tell you a few stories of how it was back then.

(Picture of Tom working maximum security, inmate visitation; back in 1997)

**FYI**- A story by Tom: I'd like to tell you a quick story, but before I do, I must warn you it's a little hard to swallow (Now that's a Corrections Officer's humor, you'll get it later in this story) in all seriousness this story is downright disgusting! Still to this day it up-sets my stomach just to tell it. I guess it's because I lived through it and still to this day it stays so freshly planted in my mind.

Okay keep in mind back in the stone age, I mean the 80s when I started this job there weren't specialized units that did cell extractions wearing the most updated protective gear with the so-called modern tools of the trade like what they have today. We went in raw maybe some of the newer rookies like myself may have had on a pair of leather gloves on but that was it. But this time we did get lucky and only because we had a sergeant with us who had a set of balls and knew how to take care of his men.

Anyway getting back to the story, there was an inmate house in the psychiatric max security unit who started to flood his cell. (For those of you that don't know this is done by the inmate clogging up the toilet and sink in his cell and running the water and repeatedly flushing the toilet.) Once we arrived on scene, the sergeant gave the order to secure water to his cell. So while we were securing the water to his cell this inmate then took baby oil and started to squirt it all over the floor then he strip down naked and started to rub the baby oil all over himself and then he took his own feces that he had early piled so conveniently on top of his mattress (and it looked like it must have taken him days to get that much) and started to cover himself in it from head to toe. Then he got on the top bunk and start to urinate all over the cell and then started yelling "I'm ready for you assholes come in and get me" while he laughed uncontrollably.

By this time we're all looking at our sergeant with looks on our faces like, if you think we're going into that cell, you're as crazy as he is. And if you would think that I couldn't make this story anymore disgusting, then it already is, here I go. Just then the foulest, most disgusting smell you can ever imagine started to work its way underneath that two inch steel door and into the hallway where we were all standing. The first and only thing that runs through your mind at that time is, one question; Dam how much stronger is that going to get once we open that cell door?

Just then the sergeant told us to follow him up to the medical unit, which I can say we all did not hesitate to do. Once we got up to medical the sergeant started to unveil his plan to us. I can still to this day remember his words exactly, as if he only said them to me/us yesterday. He said, " Unfortunately guys we have to go in there and get this scumbag crazy bastard. That's part of our job, but there's nothing that says we can't be smart in doing it" and just then he walked over to the hazmat locker and pulled out four hazmat suits (Which by the way, rumor had it, in the jail that these hazmat suits where only there for show, for when the state came in to do their inspections. The supervisors were told never to use them because of the cost involved in cleaning them.)

He pick four officers, one of which myself was included. While we were getting dressed he went over to speak to the head nurse. Once he came back he let us know exactly how it was going down. Okay guys he said "When we get back down to that cell I'm going to get the fire hose, we're then going to open up the door to that cell and I'm going to hit that crazy fucker full blast with a water shot that should put him on his ass. Once he's down, you four guys with the hazmat suits on are going to rush in. The first two guys are going to be carrying mattresses, so they can throw them down on the floor so we don't slip on the baby oil. Once you guys get close enough to him each one of you will grab a limb and secure it. Then the nurse is going to be right behind you and she's going to give him a shot of a special mixed thorazine cocktail (FYI-generic name: Chlorpromazine, is used to treat psychotic disorders such as schizophrenia or manic-depression, severe behavioral problems and aggressive behavior but given in the right dosage will knock you out cold.) which will knock him out in about ten seconds. Once he's out we'll drag him out of the cell and into the shower room where I'll finish him off, I mean clean him up with the fire hose"

The plan worked flawlessly, and thank God for those hazmat suits, gas masks and thorazine cocktails those nurses made up special for us. Now that's what I call old school, try pulling some shit like that now a days and these liberal organizations will be all over you like white on rice. The only thing that would have made that story better and safer would have been if we could have hit that inmate with a dart from a dart gun through the feeding door hatch.

Just to add to the story that was the first time I witnessed the medical staff using thorazine and whatever else it was that they put into that syringe, but this I can tell you, that stuff worked fast as hell and we used that shit on a lot of inmates Back in the Day...

(Picture of Joe in his dress blues back in 2012)

**FYI-** A story by Joe: Here's a story that happened to me one day while working the hall post. In this job as a Corrections Officer just when you start to think in your head, man things are going so smoothly today, there is a little voice that jumps out in your head and says back to you, oh yeah and this day that little voice was 100% right. A 350 pound inmate decided to screw our whole day up.

While working with three of my coworkers, we were working on getting inmates out of the holding cells for court, that's when this 350 pound inmate decided he was going to bum rush us, and of course he came straight towards me. This inmate on top of being huge and when I say 350 pounds, I'm not just talking about some big fat guy, this guy was more like the "Hulk" and was crazy as hell and very unpredictable.

Well with only a few seconds to react and being outweighed by almost 170 pounds and almost 5 inches in height and God only knows how much stronger this inmate was then me. I took out my keys (this set of keys were referred to as a bullpen set) and there were around 10 keys on that ring set, and anyone who has ever seen a key for a jail cell door knows just how big and heavy one key is let alone 10, and in trying to defend myself I hit this inmate right on top of his head as hard as I could.

Now you would think that a blow like that would have knocked most people out but not this crazy bastard. He shook his head a few times, laughed and then continued to fight us. When I tell you that we threw everything at this guy except the kitchen sink and it seem like we were fighting him for hours. We finally got his ass on the floor and handcuffed this nut job. This goes to show just how fast things can change inside a jail or prison and how quickly everything can just get out of control. Now of course this was before the days of O.C. spray, pallet balls and tasers when all you had was your fists and of course a bullpen set of keys (LOL) to protect your ass from crazy motherfuckers like this inmate.

Not that any of that modern stuff would've helped anyway because this was totally unexpected and unseen. This inmate showed no signs of making any attempt or a threat on us until after his cell door was open. And I guess the funny thing or ironic thing about this whole story is, after the four of us manage to subdue him, he apologized to us. Saying he had no idea why he bum rushed us like that.

After the shift commander who got there five minutes after this inmate was handcuffed and secured he went on to tell everyone on the shift that day that he saved our asses and we were lucky he got there just in time (Ha Ha Ha) now that's old school humor and we got our balls busted all day long by all the other officers saying "hey I heard that the old man save your ass today..."

This story just reiterates just how important it is to have each other's backs in our profession, because if I was by myself without any help that day. Who knows what would've happened. There is one thing I can tell you for sure, if that were the case. I would have had to get really dirty and let that Paterson Street mentality come out of me, maybe like a thumb in one of his eyes or even worse one of those keys, thank God my coworkers were there and I didn't have to result to doing anything close to that. You see I've never had no formal fighting or self-defense training so I would have been forced to fall back on what I learned in fighting in the streets of Paterson, New Jersey while growing up. Which was definitely one of the toughest places to grow up in the state of New Jersey and still is. So I'd like to end this story by saying to any Correction Officers out there still on the job. If you're ever in this position like this and you have no back up, just get as dirty as you need to get. After all, the name of the game is, get home to your family after your shift safe.

**FYI-** A story by Tom: Before I tell you this next story I would just like to give you a brief bio on my physical attributes so the story I'm about to tell you makes a little more sense. I started studying the martial arts when I was in the sixth grade and bounced around from school to school until I was 22 years old at which time I had finally found a school (dojo) and a system that I loved and fit me to a "T" so I stayed with it for a little over seven years. Obtaining my second degree black belt the name of the system was called Kenpo Karate and the style I studied within it was the Tiger.

But one day while I was working out in the local gym that was down the street from where I lived, I witnessed a guy bench pressing 365 pounds for three reps. I was in total amazement of his strength and decided right then and there that I was going to start powerlifting to see just how strong I could actually become. Well to make a long story short, within six years, I was bench pressing close to 600 pounds. I was ranked by powerlifting U.S.A. as the 49th strongest man in the world at that time.

Let's just say at 6'2" 345lbs I walked that jail like I owned it. As much as I'd like to be humble about this, I just have to tell the truth, I was one bad motherfucker Back in the Day. Now if anyone reading this book is or has ever worked in corrections you know as well as I do, word any word, good or bad, spreads fast, very fast throughout the entire facility. So there were many inmates who knew my story, but then again there were a handful of inmates who didn't know me from Adam. Well unfortunately for them this story is about two of those inmates who had no idea who I was or for that matter what I was capable of.

Okay, while feeding breakfast one morning an inmate reached out from behind his cell bars and stole three loafs of bread off the top of the food wagon. I let his little stunt go unaddressed until I was finished feeding the rest of the inmates on that floor. At which time, I then walked up to their cell door and told them both that I wanted the three loaves of bread back. And that if they handed them over right now the whole matter would be dropped. Their response was, "We don't know what the fuck you're talking about" I told them "I saw one of you reaching through the bars and taking them and I want them back now." Their response then was "If you want them so bad, why don't you come on in here and take them yourself."

I told them that they better just return the bread or I was going to do just that and then beat both their asses and if they tried to filing a complaint against me, I'd deny it 100%. They both just started to laugh like I had just told them the funniest joke they had ever heard. The bigger inmate said to me "We'd like to see that happen and even if it did we'd have your ass in court so fast. So fuck-you tough guy, just go back to your job, before we send you home crying to your mommy" and again they both broke out in laugher.

I told them "You both just don't get it, do you? I'm going to come in there and kick both your fucken asses, get my bread and then file charges against you both for assault on a L.E.O. (Law Enforcement Officer) and if it does go to court. I'm going to shine this badge up real pretty, put on a nice clean freshly pressed uniform, polish up my shoes and walk into the court room with a big smile on my face for all those nice people on the jury, and lie my ass off!"

Their attitude was "Yeah okay, if it wasn't for that badge you're wearing, we would kick your fucking ass right now." So I told them "What if I were to take this badge off and handed it to you and walk into your cell and shut the cell door behind me." They told me "You wouldn't have the balls to do that, and if you did we'd both would take that badge and shove it so far up your ass, you'd choke on it." Well off came the badge and I tossed it into one of their hands, walked into the cell and shut the door behind me. The look on both their faces was priceless, I wish I would've had a camera.

Well without getting into too much detail, let's just say I never had a problem with either one of those inmates ever again, or anyone else who was on that floor. Now would I ever recommend any officer now a days ever doing anything like that, absolutely NOT. But after all the title of this chapter is call "Back in the Day" and that's how we rolled back then…

**FYI**- A story by Joe: This next story I'm going to tell you about involves an officer I worked with right around the time I had just been promoted to sergeant. This officer stood about five foot two inches tall, weighed about 150 pounds soaking wet, if he was lucky and was certifiably in my mind a "Nut-job." Now before I continue I'd like to clarify one thing. I'm not characterizing this officer's physical description as anything other than to just give you a full perspective in your mind of the story. Now before I make this next statement I'd also like to add; I'm sure and I know for a fact that there are good officers out there that are of that description and in their own right are tough as nails and I wouldn't mind having them as back up in any situation. But in the same breath I would also like to tell you about a little known fact called the John Wayne syndrome. This syndrome affects some Law-Enforcement Officers and is slightly related to the Napoleon complex but doesn't necessarily fit into the category of always being consistently sided as being of small statute. The John Wayne syndrome can affect an officer who is six foot two inches tall and 250 pounds as well as it can affect in this case this officer. In a nutshell what this syndrome is all about is once an individual is given a badge he becomes superman in his own mind. Now as bad enough as that sounds, this was not this officer's only problem. He was also very immature for the job and carried absolutely no patience or working knowledge of how to work with these individual inmates on a higher level than physical, meaning using one's mental capacity to solve, avoid or understand how to deal with a potential incident.

Ok with that said on with the story:

By the time one becomes a Sergeant there are many things that you've seen in your career but this day would be different. Every department has a little crazy guy that when he does things over the years you just have to sit back and shake your head. On this day imagine this officer working in the hall area of the jail in charge of taking in new inmates and inmates that have gone to court for the day and then returning to the jail.

The first thing that this officer does with the inmate this day is of course one of the first things you're taught not to do and that is: get into a verbal back in forth with an inmate. In this case it was the usual back in forth for each talking about each other's mother's and girlfriend's in a not so great light. After the great back and forth, which of course I did not witness or I of course would have never let happen, this is what happened next.

The inmate was then searched in the search room where of course the two continue their childish back in forth. At this point the inmate was brought through a tunnel that was used to escorted said inmate back to his housing area on another floor. And you'd know that the shit talking continued, as the inmate was being moved. As they are walking through the tunnel the story changes a bit depending on who you ask but of course the bottom line is these two idiots start fighting and wrestling on the floor. Now we all know how bad this type of interaction can go bad real fast, and escorting an inmate alone is never a good idea and something I will tell you that should never be done.

Well after they fight, and mind you all done out of the range of the cameras, the two decide that, that wasn't good enough and he proceeds to escort the inmate who he just had a fight with back to his housing unit and never planned on reporting the incident. And of course that's exactly what he did and dropped him off and went back to his post and never said a word to anyone.

Next is where it gets funny! The tour commander on duty calls me and says he's been notified that an inmate was complaining he was assaulted by an officer on the first floor working the hall post when he came back from court and he mentions the name of the officer. The tour commander asks me to find out what happened. I talk to him and of course at first he stated that there was no altercation whatsoever but does admit that the two had words. At this point I then go to the floor where the inmate was housed and proceed to have a conversation with him and get the inmates story. Know as you know the stories usually have some truth and lies and you need to use common sense, facts and visual evidence when investigating a report. Much to my surprise, as I'm talking to the inmate I can see the officers badge which had made an indentation into the forehead of the inmate and I could actually read the badge number in his head, confirming the two had definitely had a physical confrontation.

Well that's all the evidence I needed to confirm this, no need to be a detective to figure this one out! Morale of the story is that he never works the hall area ever again!

**FYI-** A story by Tom: If I only had enough time or was only allowed to tell a rookie five things about this job it would be:

1- Don't ever become complacent in your work.

2- Always expect the worst to happen, but always hope for the best.

3- Always have your fellow officers back and they'll always have yours, after all the name of the game is go home safe.

4- Be consistent, fair and firm at all times and maintain a profession attitude at all times.

5- Let the inmates know that they should never confuse your kindness for weakness.

And if I had a little more time and was able to tell him or her one more thing. I'd tell them never ever to make the mistake in thinking that you know an inmate or ever trust an inmate (I know that sounds like it should be a given, but believe me a lot of officers make that mistake.) I don't care how long you've worked with an inmate or how well you think you've gotten to know an inmate. Because their personality and or situation can change like the swinging of the pendulum and you will never know it until it happens.

A perfect example of this happened to me one night at work. I had an inmate who was a trustee for me for about six months. I worked with this guy every night on an outside detail around the jail. As far as inmates go he had a pretty good attitude, never gave me a hard time, and did whatever I told him to do. And he was only sitting on an eighteen month sentence, of which he only had three more months left to serve. One of the main reasons I would have never dreamed that he would have been or turned rabbit on me (rabbit is a term used in law-enforcement referring to someone who was a runner or escaped inmate.)

This is why, what happen next caught me completely by surprise, plus I had only been on the job for a little over one year. Like I said I had this inmate on an outside detail cleaning up the parking lot in front of the Jail. I heard what sounded like a car accident, so I turned for a split second to see what happened. Just then I heard a scream coming from behind me and turned back around and he (the inmate) was coming at me like a NFL middle linebacker at full speed. Before I knew it he hit me with his shoulder right in the gut and wrapped his arms around my waist and drove me back into a car. I could feel him trying to take my handcuffs out of my handcuff case (later on I would learn he was going to try and use them as if they were a pair of brass knuckles so when he hit me with them and he would get a greater effect) as he pulled them out luckily he lost his grip on them and they went flying across the parking lot. I was also lucky because when he wrapped his arms around me they were underneath my arms. So once my back hit the car and my mind was able to focus itself and orientated on the situation at hand. My training kicked in and all of those years of studying the Martial arts paid off. I came down with a double handed knifehand shuto strike to his collarbone (for those of you who are not familiar with that term it's an open hand karate chop with both hands) this broke his grip from around my waist. I then hit him with a hammer fist to the back of his head as I kneed him in the face at the same time. I then grabbed him by his hair with both hands and dropped my weight as I pushed his face into the ground. Spinning around I then got into a full mount position on top of his back. I then ordered him to place both his hands behind his back, he didn't comply so I tried helping him out by punching him underneath both armpits, he still didn't move. A few more rights hands to his ribs and still no response.

That's when I realized I had knocked him out cold with that hammer fist to the back of the head and knee to the face. I then radioed in a 10-99 Officer needs assistance. Just then I heard the front door of the jail open up. I turned my head around to see who it was, the first of my back up had just arrived an officer who I was best friends with off the job. He ran over took out his cuffs and cuffed the inmate. Other officers soon arrived and the inmate was picked up off the ground and escorted out of the parking lot and back into the jail but not before he was thrown into the front door of the jail face first by the two officer who were escorting him.

He was secured in the main lobby of the jail until the E.M.T.'s got the ambulance and then he was brought out and placed inside the ambulance and transported to the hospital. The E.R. Dr's diagnosed him with a broken nose, broken jaw, broken collarbone, two broken ribs and a groin injury that he said he obtained from an officer while he was getting into the ambulance.

Internal affairs investigate the incident and later revealed through the investigation to me that the inmate had received a letter from home that day that his wife was leaving him and was taking his kids out of state and also wanted a divorce from him. When I.A. then asked him why he attacked me he said tell Officer Duncan I'm sorry and it was nothing personal but he had to get out of jail and stop his wife from taking his kids away from him.

Moral of the story here is you never know what's going on inside these inmates heads, my best advice to every officer is keep in mind that every inmate has the potential of becoming a ticking time bomb at any time.

**FYI-** A story by Joe: Another day on the job as Sergeant became very interesting on this day! It was a normal day in the jail, as normal as a jail gets when while supervising the first floor which covered the reception / booking area, I heard the loud screaming, a type of scream that I've never heard before coming from the strip search room! I immediately ran to the room and just opened the door not knowing what I was about to see. As a Corrections Officer that becomes normal just running into situations that you sometimes have no idea what's happening, it all just part of the job. It's something that all "Jail Guards" do not knowing if one of our co-workers are in trouble and in need of help or if it's an inmate in need of help. Well on this occasion the situation I found, thank GOD wasn't a Co-worker. When I opened the door I saw an inmate on the ground screaming in pain and as I looked down I could see his ankle dangling it was obviously broken. And I should say that the two Officers working that post that day I knew very well.

The first thing I did upon my arrival right after my initial assessment of the situation was to call Central Control immediately and request medical assistance, medical attention came swiftly. And while they were attending to the inmate's medical needs, I asked the two officers if they were ok, they seemed physically sound but both were a bit in shock as I could tell by the looks on their faces. I then took the one officer aside who I trust with my life, and asked him "what the hell just happened?" He explained that while strip searching this inmate, who I later found to be an "Immigration inmate" who was housed in our facility and just coming back from court. While he was dressing back into his jail issued clothes from his court clothes he became very belligerent to the officers instructions. On several occasions he was ordered to behave, keep his mouth shut and he would be advised what to do next. It was at this point that things went from bad to real bad the inmate threw a punch at the one of the officers and after that all hell broke loose.

While the Officers were trying to control this inmate, the inmate then made a fatal mistake and caused his own injury. You see in the strip room there are metal partitions so that each inmate cannot be seen by the other inmates while stripping, this is for privacy reasons. Well while attempting to kick the officer the inmate missed his target and ended up kicking the metal partition and breaking his ankle in half causing him excruciating pain thus the screaming that sent me running in the first place.

I'll be totally honest with you, at this point I only truly cared about knowing that my officers were OK. So at this point knowing that, I just stay there to supervise the medical attention that the nurse was giving to this inmate and instructed my officers to take a coffee break so they could get their composure back and then write their reports. The inmate was soon taken to the hospital and treated.

As you are well aware and could speculate, the inmate had a much different story about what transpired but in my mind, the officer I talked to first, who to me was very professional and trustworthy gave the truthful story about what took place in that room. And as you can guess the two officers were scrutinized and vetted by the internal affairs division who eventually reported that the officers were at no fault but that was after a very lengthy investigation.

Of course the civil liberty attorneys, who have never even met an inmate that they haven't liked or believed in, ran with the lies told by this inmate. That's when of course all the major news agencies showed up and ran with the story also. The inmate was then removed eventually from our facility because of course he claimed he would be targeted.

Being known as one of the toughest jails in the country at that time, many inmates made up stories to get out of our facility and the immigration detainees were the biggest complainers and pains in the asses. If it wasn't making the county so much money to house these detainees after 9-11, they were more trouble than they were worth as far As I was concerned, but they paid the bills.

Eventually the officers were exonerated by all and the detainee was sent back to his country and deported. He did however before he left filed a federal civil rights lawsuit naming President Clinton, Janet Reno, our Sheriff, and the two officers involved as defendants. The lawsuit of course was without merit. But that's a quick story about how things can go ugly real fast and how writing great accurate reports goes a long way to keeping you out of the courts and safe to go home to your family!

Kudos to the Sheriff at the time, he always backed his officers when allegations from inmates came forward. Moral at this, "write accurate and detailed reports" and it always helps to have a Sheriff who has your back when shit like this happens.

**FYI-** A story by Tom: In this next story I'm about to tell you I'm going to take a look at the lighter side of corrections. As much as our job is serious and life-and-death is always just around the corner. A Corrections Officer will always find time no matter how stressful the day can be to have a little stress relief between officers (AKA breaking each other's balls or pulling a prank on one another.)

Most Corrections Officers have a very unique sense of humor. Now what is, and should be a given; and everyone should know is that every rookie is going to get their balls busted, sent on wild goose chases and set up by other Officers to go and ask ranking supervisors the most stupidest questions. But when you're dealing with a seasoned Officer you need to become more creative and believe me the creative mind of a Corrections Officer is limitless. Now I could write an entire book on this subject alone, so for the sake of trees and ink I'll limit it to just too short stories or should I say pranks.

I had this officer or as we called ourselves down in Florida at the time Deputy Sheriffs who I was very close with. We were constantly going back-and-forth pranking each other with the craziness of stunts, just to break the tension while at work. I'll also add that we were the two lead characters that would generate most of the ball busting on every new rookie. And that's exactly how this first prank I'm going to tell you about started. We had just started our shift with this new kid who had just gotten out of the academy. We were working the midnight shift and we were riding him hard busting his balls, sending him to the sergeant with all kinds of stupid shit. Well I had just gotten back to my post from lunch, I guess you can call it lunch even though it was like at 3 o'clock in the morning. When my old dear buddy AKA best friend set me up. I just walked in the control room and he informed me that this rookie that we were going at all night long was trying to get even with me. I asked him what he meant by that and he told me that he took my briefcase taped it up to a chair and put it in the middle of the abandoned room of the old sergeants office that was next to our control room.

Well right off the bat I was a little suspicious first wondering if this was my buddy trying to set me up or if this rookie actually had the balls to try and go after a veteran officer. So I walked over to the old sergeants office, opened the door and sure enough there in the middle of the empty room sat a chair with my briefcase taped to it. I walked up to the chair gave it the once over and even kicked it to tip it over. Nothing had happened and as I was un-taping my briefcase from it and thinking to myself how stupid this was and how I was going to get him back. The door to the office slammed shut and a ventilation fans turned on and through the duct vents that were on the ceiling came down a white powdery substance that covered the entire room, myself included. When I tell you I looked like Frosty the Snowman it's no exaggeration. I walked over open the door and to my surprise there was my "Best Buddy" the sergeant, and about five other officers laughing their balls off.

Okay so now my buddy was one up on me. What he actually did was took a whole bunch of powdered coffee creamer and put it in the vents so when I walked in the room to un-tape my briefcase, shut the door and he turned on the ventilation system, out came about 5 pounds of powdered coffee creamer all over the place; ok funny, funny I thought now game on, my turn.

You heard that saying, patience is a virtue? Well it took me a while and after about a good 6 to 8 months of everyone calling me Deputy Frosty my turn came. It was Thanksgiving I had my buddy over the house for dinner. I don't know how many bottles of wine we drank but we were both pretty well lit-up. Now my buddy thought he was an up-and-coming country western star singer. He had wrote this song for his wife so titled "The garden love song." And he wasn't really sure if it was good or not. Well I finally convinced him to let me videotape him so he could see it and hear it from my perspective. Which I did and we watched it and I tried to convinces him how good it was. But there was a method to my madness and my motive. The following night when I went into work I pulled our lieutenant aside. Told him that I need his help and wanted to repay my buddy for the incident that happened with the coffee powder. He asked me my plan and agreed to it.

This is how it went down. We're all at roll-call one night and at the end, the Lieutenant says we have a quick training video everyone needs to watch before we hit the floors. Well needless to say it wasn't a training video it was my buddy sitting on my couch, playing my guitar and singing that love song for the whole shift to watch. I'll tell you the look on his face was priceless it was worth the 6 to 8 months of hell I went through as Deputy Frosty. His song brought down the house standing ovation's for his video and yells for an encore didn't stop for weeks...

Those are just too little stupid stories that happened between officers all the time inside the walls. As serious as our job is and the games we all play with each other the camaraderie and friendships that come together with the job and bonds that are made between friends last forever...

**FYI-** A story by Joe: One of the first days after I was promoted to Sgt. of course I would be involved in several incidents. The first had to do with a female prisoner on her way to be shipped to prison and was being pat searched and printed out before leaving our facility. Now keep in mind that in many facilities the female inmates are far more of a problem as far as discipline and acting out than their male counterparts! Throughout my career I've tried to never put my hands on a female prisoner but remember you must protect yourself, your coworkers and other inmates at times so you may not have no other choice than to do so. A Coworker once said to me, "I don't enjoy it but if you have a female inmate acting like a man then you have no other choice but to treat them like one." That being said I walked into the area where the females were being shipped and I witnessed a female inmate wrestling on the ground and kicking one of my female officers, I ran to her aid yelling for her to stop. The inmate continued to kick and throw punches after I gave her a direct order to stop. At this point I grabbed the inmate by the back of her shirt and as I began to push and place her up against the wall towards the cell doors she tried to get out from my grip and fell into the door. At this point I secured her arms and with the assistance of the female officer we placed her into handcuffs. I looked up at this point and much to my surprise the prisoner cut her forehead up pretty bad against the doors and was bleeding like I've never seen anyone bleed before. Of course she was screaming and of course threatening to call her lawyer. I of course could care less who she wanted to call I was just interested in getting her to the nurse and get treated and because of her actions she would not be getting shipped to state prison that day but would be on her way to the emergency room for stitches. You see you never want this type of interaction with an inmate while you're preparing for work but in our business unfortunately this is part of our daily business. So my first day on the job as a Sergeant was eventful and took much of my time writing detailed reports about what had transpired. Quick note on this incident a temporary employee who was not even present during the incident but worked in the female section kept spreading rumors that myself and the female officer were at fault during the incident and based on her own words was terminated from employment because of the lies she was telling about what had taken place.

Eventually the inmate required 40 stitches and was charged criminally for aggravated assault on an officer and found guilty of the same in court. So male or female you have no idea how they are going to act and what may come your way during your shift.

Bottom line you do what you have to do to protect your co- workers and yourself from harm regardless of the gender. Now remember in our business something like this takes hours of your time writing reports, reviewing the reports of the officers involved and making corrections when needed. Countless of hours of talking to the dreaded Internal Affairs (just kidding) to give them your version of what took place. Remember all the reports you write and submit can and eventually make it to court so take them seriously. Nothing worse than getting in front of a slick defense attorney and you've written a subpar report and have left out many details. Once you do that it will surely be your last time after the embarrassment you will endure in front of the jury and judge. Countless hours talking to your attorney also preparing for court. So you see it's not as simple as getting the job done and going home, there is plenty of hard work in between and what you'll discover is the better the supervisor handling the investigation and how thorough they are the better off you'll be in any incident! That is something I definitely took pride in while preparing and helping others to prepare their reports.

**FYI-** A story by Tom: This next and last story I'm about to tell you is so very personal and hard for me to tell; because it involves an officer that my wife and I were best friends with and not only him but also with his wife for over 30 years. It's truly heart breaking for me to tell because of how close my wife and I are with him and his whole family, to this day I for the life of me cannot figure out the why's and how's of it and how he let it happen.

I guess I'll start it off by saying this officer (let's call him Officer Billy) at the time of this story had close to 21 years on the job and in my opinion was and is a very smart man and one I always thought of as a guy who knew the job very well and was well aware of how officers can be and are manipulated my inmates. This officer had a very strong personality, a great family life, kids and a wife who was/is a beautiful woman, he came from a law-enforcement family and like I said had a very sharp sense about the job. I'd also like to add that over the years that I knew him we had many close man to man conversations about as you can imagine almost very topic possible. We would talk a lot about work, sports, family matters, vacations we wanted to go on next with the families together and so many, many more things, but one thing we never talked about as do a lot of man was other women, we both were very happy and secure with our marriages. That's why still to this day I cannot believe this story is true and this happened to my close friend. Ok you can probably guess where this story is going by now.

One night while my wife and I were sitting in our living room watching T.V. the phone rang; it was Officer Billy's wife. Now one thing I should have added was I was already retired and Officer Billy worked as a Corrections Officer for a difference department than the one I was retired from at the time of this phone call. Right off the bat I could tell by the look on my wife's face that something was wrong and I already knew from the caller ID on the T.V. who the call was from so my concern jump immediately. My wife's next words were (let's call her Sally) it's Sally she wants me to put the phone on speaker so she can talk to both of us. My heart without even hearing her first words already skipped a beat when I hear my wife say that.

The next thing I heard Sally say was you guys are not going to fucken believe this shit. Then she paused for a second which seemed like minutes or even hours as my wife and I just looked at each other with looks like OH MY GOD this is going to be bad. Sally then said: "Billy just came home from work and informed me that I.A. (Internal Affairs) just suspended him and he's under investigation for four counts, one being sexual contact with a female inmate and that has been going on for over a year now."

Needless to say our jaws hit the ground and we (my wife and I) were in total shock and disbelief. We just sat there listening unable to say anything while we listened to Sally tell us what had/was going on. It was so surreal like it was a bad joke being played on us. My first thoughts were no way, not Billy, not with a female inmate; a sexual affair.

This is the guy I had countless conversations with and knew them so well, I knew just how much he loved his wife, never ever did he even talk about other women with me (and if you're a guy reading this you know what I'm talking about) this guy never showed NO interest in any other women not that I ever picked up on and we were tight, we talked about everything. This guy was in my opinion one of the finest officers I knew, a guy who knew his job well, all aspect of it, knew all the "GAMES" played by inmates and he did his job well. A top-notch professional in my opinion. How could this have happen to him? It's just not right, it makes NO SENSE and to add just one more unbelievable incredible fact this female inmate was a very high-profile maximum-security inmate awaiting a trial on first-degree premeditated murder.

Ok without disclosing anymore facts about this; I'd like to now get into the how's and why's of how this matter came to be and how it happens to so many officers in corrections. But Before I continue any further I'd like to touch on two very interesting words that should be in every Correction Officers vocabulary and work attitude: empathy and sympathy.

Both words have similar usage, but differ in their emotional meaning.

**Empathy** is the ability to mutually experience the thoughts, emotions, and direct experience of others. Empathy is the experience to be able to understand another person's condition from their perspective. You place yourself in their shoes and feel what they are feeling.

**Sympathy,** is the ability in which there is a feeling of care and understanding for the suffering of others. Acknowledging another person's emotional hardships and providing comfort and assurance. Feelings of pity and sorrow for someone else's misfortune it's a feeling that you care about and are sorry about someone else's trouble, grief, misfortune, etc. A feeling of support for something or someone.

Ok with that said, here is where it goes wrong for so many Correction Officers. In our job its ok to have empathy for an inmate or inmates, as a matter of fact it will most likely make you a better Corrections Officer. But it's when that officer crosses the line over into sympathy that he or she is headed into big trouble and many inmates try and do just that. It's a tactic use by classic manipulators and with the very good ones it's very hard to see it coming. Not that I'm trying to make an excuse for my friend, he broke the first rule of corrections. Never move from a professional relationship into a friendly one with any inmate thus the Empathy and Sympathy concept of a Correction Officers paradigm of his work environment and his feeling and actions he needs to work with to maintain a professional relationship with inmates.

A classic manipulator knows that once they can move you into that sympathy stage from the empathy stage you've just become a "Sitting Duck." And unfortunately for so many officers by the time they realize it even if they do realize it, it's too late. They're like the fish on the hook being reeled into a net.

Now motives for inmates using these manipulative tactics on officers varies from the need of the inmate. In most cases it's to try and get an officer to start bringing in contraband or even in some extreme cases to aid in an escape plan.

If I had to put a moral to this story it's: as a Corrections Officer you should NEVER let your guard down, always be vigilant even when you're engaging in what you believe is just small talk with an inmate. Always remember these inmates have eight hours every day to watch you, to get to know you, to hear you talk with other officers. They know you better than you think they do and anything they say or do in front of you is mostly done 99.9 % of the time with some type of motive to benefit themselves. And above all things NEVER think that you're too smart, to have a stupid inmate get one over on you because your first mistake is thinking that all inmates are stupid when in fact a lot of them will have higher I.Q.'s then you…

**FYI-** A story by Joe: For my final story I'm going to change the pace a bit and write a bit on the spirit and character of the Corrections Officers, I've been associated with over my 25 years in service.

This will not come to any surprise to the many Corrections Officers all over the world reading this, but if you've ever needed help or a disaster has fallen upon you, you will have no greater helper than the Corrections Officer. From raising money for underprivileged children and families to raising money for sick and dying children whenever called upon. On many occasions my fellow workers gave their hard earned money for charity and most of all they give up their valuable time with their families to help the less fortunate. And it's not just a few, I'm speaking of get into any difficulty and if disaster strikes you will be flooded with officers willing and able to help.

Every Christmas was a time where a school was picked and donations of toys were raised and many children, smiles on their faces were met by the officers and Santa Claus giving gifts and creating smiles and lasting memories for these children. The school was picked from the inner city where the children needed it the most and there is no better feeling than seeing a smile on the face of our children in this world.

With all the bad press the corrections community gets and law enforcement in general it's important to recognize the many great things we do in our communities, with our own hard earned money and our valuable time that is most of the time over looked.

I can't tell you how many times I've seen officers reaching in their pockets for money to help fire victims, flood victims and victims of crimes and natural illnesses.

This is the story of hope and goodwill that I've seen and my coworkers have seen and grown accustomed to and is no big deal to witness, it's a way of life we chose to help others in need and is most of the time done without praise and nothing is expected back. This is the story that I knew I had to share with the public and it's the most important thing we do in our lives. This is the story the politicians and the press won't tell you about because it's not gonna sell newspapers or get a politician any votes. It's the few bad things, the mistakes that they choose to share and that's a shame on them. I prefer to share the positive things we do which of course happen way more times a day then the few mistakes.

As departments and union leaders realize getting this positive message out only garners more respect for our line of work. I hope many more civilians will see the great things you guys do every day for your fellow constituents. For this I have the utmost respect for our profession and will stake us up with anyone when it comes to helping others in need! I simply say Thank You and keep up the great work you do!

The Perfect Back in the Day Picture...

(A pic of set of Old School Cell keys as seen on the front cover of the book, the more popular keys now a days & commonly used are made by the Folger Adams Company.)

# CHAPTER 10

---

*With Friends like these, who needs ENEMIES!*

---

In this chapter Joe and I will discuss <u>all the help and support</u> Corrections Officers <u>get and have gotten</u> from politicians, (AKA their bosses and you should know, this only applies in certain departments across the country) especially on the local level such as Sheriff's Departments. We will also discuss how they (politicians) <u>truly care about the Corrections Officer</u> and how it's not always all about themselves and making sure that they're reelected to office. Also how the administration is always looking out for and backing the Correction Officers up 100%...

We're sorry this chapter was so long (LOL.) This will conclude the end of chapter ten. We hope you enjoyed reading about **ALL THE HELP and SUPPORT** Correction Officers get.

\*\* Now don't get us wrong with the point we're trying to make with this chapter. There are MANY Sheriffs, Corrections Commissioners and Wardens who are great to work for and who do have the backs of their officers 100% (NOTE: and their NOT the ones we're talking about.) But unfortunately there are a significant amount of departments out there that do exist, in which this chapter applies. Thus the need for us to have this chapter in our book.

# CHAPTER 11

## *Sex Behind The Bars*

This chapter deals with every kind of sexual act you can think of that happens behind the bars and not only what most think "RAPE." Let's face it the first word or thought that most people think of when they think about Jail or Prison is "RAPE."

They envision some big scary guy or a group of guys raping someone. As a matter of fact (if you're NOT a Correctional Officer) we're like 99.9% sure that this was one of the first thoughts you had, when you first saw this book.

So here it comes; SEX BEHIND THE BARS (and it's NOT pretty)... and whether it's consensual or not, we all know it happens.

Let's start out with the so called good news, if you can call it that. First off here are a few facts that you might not be aware of. And contrary to popular belief almost 90% of every sexual act behind the bars that is committed in a correctional facilities is consensual. And out of that 90% in 80% of those cases, these men do not see themselves committing a so called "gay act." or for that matter see themselves as being gay.

The paradigm that drives this logic is that since incarceration prohibits the natural course or action a heterosexual male would normally take to fulfill their sexual desires is impossible, and that knowing they would not normally turn to such an act and that their first and only choice on the outside would be a woman. This <u>justifies</u> in their minds that they're forced and warranted only by their circumstances to do whatever it take to fulfill their sexual needs and desires, thus making it an acceptable act in their minds. And they will let you know that this action is only acceptable, ONLY in Jail or Prison...

Now moving on to the other 10% of sexual acts that happen in correctional facilities, Non-Consensual Sex (RAPE.) Yes it happens, unfortunately that's the one thing that Hollywood gets right in their movies. This act happens for one of two reasons: the first reason is to punish someone and in these cases a large percentage of the time there usually is an object that takes on the role of the rape and not another male... In the second case the rape takes place because of a physical attraction one inmate has for another. Now is this case the victim is "usually" smaller, younger & weaker than the perpetrator committing the act. But in the cases where the victim might be seen as someone who can and will put up a fight that just one perpetrator might not be able to handle him. For these cases there are two ways of dealing with this: one is that the perpetrator will find other inmates/prisoner who would enjoy raping this victim with him thus resulting in a gang rape. The other way is the perpetrator simply paying off other inmate to help him rape the victim...

Unfortunately there is one more scenario that fits into this chapter: Officer Inmate sex and that happens with female officers on male inmates, male officers on female inmates, female officers on female inmate, male officers on male inmates and even rape cases in all those ways... That's just a fact in life, because just like in any other professions there are bad apples... Men & women who give their colleagues a bad name...

With all that said we (Joe & I) can say that we either have saw or heard of all of these happening at one time or another during our careers. There have been many inmates charged & officers fired because of this...

Now without getting into that much detail we're going to try and give you a true sense of this disgusting act (problem) that every single person in the world knows happens behind the bars, and it's once again something that falls on the Correction Officers shoulders at work and must be handled in a professional matter and what goes unsaid is, this act along with all the other unspeakable acts this profession has especially if witnessed (and believe us if you make a career in corrections there won't be too many things that you won't witness that are in this book) this will be something that each Correction Officer will have sketched into the back of their mind along with all the other bull-shit they see for the rest of their lives...

Hopefully everyone reading this can understand that there is just something about seeing, another man on top of another man, or witnessing a rape, thus we do not need to explain to you why so many Correction Officers don't talk about it.

Ok so without further ado here we go: The first time I (Tom) saw another man on top of another man I was thrown into what I think was complete an utter shock for about 10 or 15 seconds. I just stood there eyes open wide and I think my jaw hit the floor. When I snapped back to reality I was still lost for words... What the fuck should I say/what the fuck should I do, was the first two thoughts that ran through my mind... I'll tell you what, the academy never trained me for this moment... So I yelled out the first think that came to my mind, which was "What the fuck are you two jerk-offs doing" They both just stopped and looked at me and said nothing. It was like I was stuck in the twilight zone, seconds felt like hours. All we did was stare at each other, well after about I guess 10 or 15 seconds. I just walked away... The whole time thinking and arguing to myself; you just can't walk away from that, I first thought. Then answering myself, well what the fuck do you want me to do? Go back and pull them ass-holes apart, I'm NOT touch those two fucking guys... You got to do something I said to myself, then I answered myself back real quick, oh yeah says who! Fuck that... was my last and finale thought along with: I'm not writing no report about two guys fucking, I wish I'd never even saw that, all I wanted to do is forget about it (well I can tell you now, that happen about 25 years ago and I can still see it in my mind like it was yesterday.)

I lived with that for a long time, not telling anyone and it bothered me a lot (thinking back now about it I should have found a superior whom I trusted and talk to him or her about it.) But back in those days Corrections and Correction Officers had a whole different persona. Officers were macho, tough, strong and able to handle ANYTHING... We didn't have anything that bothered us, we just sucked up everything and moved on (plus who would you talk to, departments back then didn't provide anyone for officers to talk too and who would want to because that would only make you look weak.)

Well Thank God times have changed and these officers today know better and have resources available to them. They're taught in the academy that there is no shame in seeking out help to talk with someone about the problems you encounter on the job.

Then there were other times that I could hear a rape taking place and you can tell just by knowing what that type of scream or screams sound like (It's kinda hard to explain, I guess only other Correction Officers really can know what we're talk about here, when we say you know just by hearing that type of scream.) But 99 out of 100 times, by the time you're able to get there, it's over already and you know dam well 99% of the time the victim is not going to tell you what just happy, because that's like signing his death warrant.

The last thing you want to do as an Inmate is rat on another inmate… You're better off trying to take care of it yourself or if you tell (Ratting them out) than hoping you're moved to a segregated section such as protective custody (and FYI even that's not guaranteed to be 100% safe.) There is just one last thing I want to say about this and that is about that "SCREAM" it's a God awful wrenching scream, just another thing that once a Correction Officer comes to know, it will live with him or her forever…

Only one time in my 25 years was it ever brought to my (Joe) attention that a rape had taken place and it came from inmates inside the very dorm that it happen in. The allegation was that one inmate was forced to have sex with another inmate. And let me say right off the bat that among all of the allegations and crimes that can be committed within a correctional facility, rape is at the top of the list that no Corrections Officer wants to ever hear about. And in this case it was alleged to had happen in a dorm with 60 other inmates watching. That's why I wasn't at first quick to believe it either way.

But being a Capt. at the time I knew that I would have to order an investigation and notify all the proper authorities of the allegation of rape.

The inmate being accused was one of the most feared inmates in our facility by other inmates and very well known to the staff. He was an inmate that was highly prone to use violence on other inmates, and always used a shank (knife.) He was someone that always had to be handled with great attention by the staff because he was so unpredictable and dangerous.

So the first thing I order of course is that alleged victim be sent to the hospital to be medically evaluated and that the alleged perpetrator of the crime be interviewed.

Now in this case even though the victim was smaller & weaker than the perpetrator committing the alleged act, and only because it was said to take place in an open dorm with 60 other inmates watching. My first impression was, would this inmate really no matter how tough he was, really rape and assault another inmate out in the open in a dorm with 60 other inmates watching?

Well much to my surprise, this inmate actually admitted during the interview that, yes, he raped this other inmate and a few hours later the hospital report confirmed it.

It's was a situation that most of us who were there at the time didn't think would have turned out the way it did, but it just goes to show what an unpredictable and dangerous profession we chose and the seriousness of the job we have.

The bottom line here is a Correction Officers always needs to stay alert and never jump to conclusions; because just when you think sometime happened because of something, or it didn't happen because of something, you just might find out otherwise. Because like no other profession in the world shit hits the fan real fast in this business.

My reason to tell this story is to highlight the fact that coming into work on any day of the week, things can become very serious and dangerous.

Before we end this chapter we both would like to say: There are many different opinions that people (the public) have about rape inside a correctional facility. Some people will come straight out and tell you. "Oh well shit happens, and if that scumbag didn't commit a crime in the first place he wouldn't be there. So maybe it's a just punishment and he's getting just what he deserves." Where on the other hand many people see it for the crime that it really is, a vicious, physical, horrible, atrocity that no one ever deserves.

And as a Correction Officer we're not there to judge anyone. We're there to maintain the three C's: Care, Custody and Control. And any, and all crimes, against any inmate falls under CARE and we as professionals are sworn to uphold that.

# CHAPTER 12

## *When it finally sinks in*

A t the Start of our (Tom & I) careers and I'm sure it's true with about 99% of all Correction Officers (Rookie's) that are fresh out of the academy. You will have a totally different view of the inmate population at the beginning of your career, then you will have at the end of your career.

Thoughts at first like: they're the enemy, they're stupid, they need to be punished & you'll make sure that happens, they're ALL scumbags and so many more... Well at first a lot of young officers feel that's the way and that's how they need to act around them. Well after a few years of arguing and such with them and really getting to know them and all the different types of inmates it will start to sink in for you as it did for us that they are just people who are for the most part are just job security and that not all of them are bad people. There are a lot who just made bad/dumb choices in life at a young age or maybe while drunk or on drugs. Now don't gets us wrong we're not trying to make excuses for their crimes we're just making a reference to their character while they're incarcerated. And once you start to realize this you may even sometimes think less of some of your fellow officers at times who really have no idea how to act with them.

Ok let's say it again: Now don't get us wrong, there are many, many inmates who are worthless to society by their own actions and deeds and deserve very little respect from us, and are true scumbags, believe us when we say you'll know who they are. But then again on the other hand there are also many that don't want to give us a hard time and they know that they need us for the many things they need to make their lives safe and to make sure that they are given the things from us to live the best life they can while incarcerated. Now it's our job to figure out the two different types of inmates and how to manage our days accordingly with them so we can put the least amount of stress on ourselves. Trust us, (and the sooner you do the better off you'll be) fighting and arguing with inmates who have nothing better to do is counterproductive to your wellbeing and I'm sure theirs also, but a lot of those type of inmates don't even give a shit. So guess what? It's just a game sometimes for them to just fuck with you...

Ok the trick here or better yet we should say the smart thing here to do is work smart every day and most of those days can and will be good ones for you. Now don't get us wrong, we were never the so called soft officer who allowed inmates to run their days the way they wanted too and also run us into the ground. If you're a firm but fair officer who the inmates also know takes no shit from anyone and you're still professional in doing your job you'll get the utmost respect from "MOST" of the inmate population and trust us, we know this for a fact!

Again let us say you will "ALWAYS" have that inmate/inmates (and sometimes on some days more than you'd like to have) who could care less, and for him/them they deserve no respect from you and will suffer the consequences of their actions. Bottom line: is to be firm, fair and level headed with these inmates and show them and tell them on a daily basis that it's the officer that runs the correctional institution "It's OUR HOUSE our RULES!" But also be that type of officer that's not there to break their balls, but you're also not there to take and won't take any shit from "ANY ONE OF THEM" and when they disrespect you and when the rules aren't followed you're prepared to do your job without fear and you're smart enough to do it the right way and make sure that they know that they're not ever going to ever win.

Now just remember you will come across the officer (most of the time a newer one but then again there is always that dumb ass one who never learned what we're now talking about in this chapter) who could care less how you feel about running your floor or section. That's why it's so important and depends on us, the senior officers to pave the way for these younger guys who are just coming up, mostly to let them know the correct way of doing things, tell them what you've learned (the smart ones WILL listen) over time and teach them all the mistakes you made so they don't make the same ones.

Like we said the smart ones will understand that after all, you've put in the time, sweat and tears so they don't have to, learn the things you're trying to teach them on their own. And we're sure, no we know that there will be those young officer that will think and maybe even have the balls to tell you to your face that you're just getting soft in your old age. But tell them that's not the case, you're working smarter these days. Let them know that's the most important thing that they can ever learn, coming to work every day, working smart not hard, working in a safe environment and getting home to your family with a clear head from a stress free day, remember 99% of the inmate population wants the same thing you do and has no problems with the rules. It's up to us the professional Corrections Officer to see that the place is run that way.

We spend many days and nights working in an job that is dangerous and sometimes exciting in many different ways GOOD and BAD and if you're lucky you'll have 25 years like I've had the pleasure of doing. It's a job that we hear all too often from our fellow officers everyday about hoping to retire and telling us to the minute how much longer they have left on the job.

For me this happened the last year of my career in Corrections and it was very bittersweet. Yes I was happy, I was leaving unscathed and free from the violence some have been unlucky to have put upon them. At by no means did I go thru my career without many ups and downs, problems and accomplishments, that's the life in our business, you can be on top one day and it can bring you down just as fast.

But if we are lucky the day will come where we can sit back and realize that there's finally a light at the end of the tunnel. And for me, when I did I was both very excited to start the new chapter in my life. And also very sad and almost had a feeling I would like to stay a bit longer, you see, as you in our profession know, we share a bond with our brothers and sisters that cannot be matched, the real heroes other than our parents who have done so much for us.

So that being said, when that day finally came for me, of course it brought a tear and a smile on my face. Knowing that would be the last time I put that uniform on and saw those heroes faces, walking through the facility. Just writing this now I've had a tear and smile just thinking about it. It was a tough day for sure.

But I will say, looking back and now many exciting things ahead I'm grateful to the corrections profession and my department (Passaic County Sheriff's Department) for allowing me to be involved in and allowing me to grow into the man I am today. Remember this is a great life and we have the opportunity to share it, and after retirement we get to love and embrace it even more.

My attitude today is one of, live everyday like it's your last. Play hard, love hard and never have any regrets in life. Do this without exception and smile every day. Smile knowing you were a Corrections Officer, part of the greatest and most honorable profession that most cannot understand, except the true heroes in my mind, the Corrections Officer! Wow!

In addition PLEASE: **Stop and Think about this:**

A problem can't be solved unless it's heard and in order for something to be heard you must talk...

Suicide, P.T.S.D., Drug Addiction and Alcoholism are just some of the major problems that are alive and well within this profession and even in retirees...

Do your loved ones a big favor, if you are someone, or know someone, who needs help, GET IT...

Contact the appropriate people who can help, and know that you are not alone... No problem or situation is worth destroying your life or ending your life over...

Think of your loved ones, the only solution they want to your problem is you well and with them...

**Safe Call Now:**

Safe Call Now is a **CONFIDENTIAL**, comprehensive, 24 hour crisis referral HOT LINE for all public safety employees and their family members nationwide.

Safe Call Now is a FREE resource for public safety employees to speak confidentially with officers, former law enforcement officers, public safety professionals and/or mental healthcare providers who are familiar with your line of work.

**Phone #** - 206-459-3020
**Website**: www.SafeCallNow.org

(Picture of Joe (Left) & Tom (Right) doing a promotion for the book, on the radio show " Tier Talk.")

# A FINAL NOTE

The main reason we wrote this book: was to correct Hollywood's version of what they call "Jail Guards" or "Prison Guards" and to show/tell everyone who reads this book that "WE" (Correction Officers) are TRUE Law-Enforcement Professionals who put our lives on the line each day...

We would just like to leave you with this one last thought. There are places in this country where societies worst nightmares live and where the best of Man (Correction Officers) & the worst of Man (Inmates/Prisoners) face off and try to get through each day alive; these place are called Prisons & Jails and those nightmares are REAL and the Men & Women who keep them there, are called Correction Officers and NOT Guards, NOT Glorified Babysitter, NOT want to be cops, NOT Screws, NOT Hacks and NOT Turnkeys.

We're also tired of being looked at as the Redheaded Step Child of Law-Enforcement. So please pay us the RESPECT we DESERVE and have EARNED as the professionals we are.

We're CALLED Correction Officers and we're the fucken Toughest and Baddest Law-Enforcement Officers GOD ever made...

We would like to dedicate this book to all the Retired & Active Correction Officers who have and are putting their lives on the line to keep societies most dangerous individuals secure.

And to those of you who enjoyed reading a book that finally showed respect for the Correction Officer, in the light of truth (as the true Law-Enforcement Officers & Professionals we are.) We would like to ask you to share a review of this book on one of your social media pages...

Thanks & God Bless you all,
Joe DeFranco & Tom Duncan

Made in the USA
Middletown, DE
22 September 2019